The Roots of a
Christian Civilization

FR. BRIAN THOMAS BECKET MULLADY, O.P., S.T.D.

THE ROOTS

OF A

CHRISTIAN CIVILIZATION

First Principles of a Just and Ordered Society

EWTN Publishing, Inc.
Irondale, Alabama

Dedicated to
The Dominican Sisters of St. Cecilia
The Dominican Sisters of Mary, Mother of the Eucharist
The Carmelite Sisters of the Most Sacred Heart of Los Angeles

Contents

THE ROOTS OF A
CHRISTIAN CIVILIZATION

Introduction

"Man is by nature a social animal." This quotation from Aristotle's *Politics* is one of the oldest statements concerning human nature in Western civilization. The affirmation that human beings can only attain their perfection within a social context is a truth which reason teaches through human observation and has also been constantly affirmed by the Catholic Church. The Lord Himself taught that human beings should love one another.

For thousands of years, the exact origin and nature of society has been a matter of intense speculation and debate. Questions concerning human freedom, authority, work, and business are among the more basic questions human beings discuss. There is a rich literature in the ancient world about the ideal society and the principles of social conduct. These were made more prolix in the discussions in Western society during the Enlightenment, which eventually gave rise to the Western democracies as we know them today. The question of society's nature has great importance for morals. Should law implement morality or not? Things like abortion, euthanasia, gay marriage, and socialized medicine are rampant today, and more and more receive the blessing of civil law, even in countries traditionally considered to be Catholic.

Catholic politicians seem oblivious to the social doctrine of the Church when casting their votes for legislation that destroys the very moral fiber of the nation, especially as it reflects on the promotion of the family. Some of the clergy seem equally fuzzy on just what moral actions they should be catechizing the faithful about. The laity seem even more at sea about what the Church teaches on many social matters. When a pope condemns unrestricted capitalism, this is identified with socialism, even though other popes who were great opponents of socialism have taught the same thing. Democracies seem to have adopted the point of view that majority rule creates ethics with no nod made to objective human nature.

C. S. Lewis reflected on this in *The Screwtape Letters* when he has a senior tempter in Hell say to a junior tempter on earth: "*Democracy* is the word with which you must lead them by the nose.... It will never occur to them that *Democracy* is properly the name of a political system, even a system of voting, and that this has only the most remote and tenuous connection with what you are trying to sell them. Nor, of course, must they ever be allowed to raise Aristotle's question: whether 'democratic behaviour' means the behaviour that will preserve democracy."[1]

Traditional Catholic thought very clearly teaches basic principles that explain the origin and nature of society. These principles have important applications related to things like the nature of government and its role in the formation of conscience, the development of a just economic climate, the relation of Church and State, the nature and

---

[1] C. S. Lewis, *The Screwtape Letters* (New York: Macmillan Publishing Company, 1961), 197.

defense of the family, and finally, the right to life. Countless papal teachings have been employed to explicate and apply these principles to modern society since the original papal encyclical about economics confronting both Marxism and capitalism, *Rerum Novarum*, was issued by Pope Leo XIII on May 19, 1891.

When I was a young seminarian studying theology in the early '70s, I took a class in history of the Church from a devout Catholic professor from the University of California, Berkeley. He stated that though he read *Rerum Novarum* in his Catholic high school, it always seemed something which was too little, too late, and had no real application to social thought. This attitude is sadly reflected in the general opinion of many Catholics today about all of papal social teaching. If it does not seem radical enough, it simply seems out of touch with the culture. Part of the reason people think this is perhaps that they really do not understand all that is at issue in papal teaching contained in the social encyclicals of the past 125 years. These teachings are the result of a development of many principles which come from both Scripture and Tradition. In many cases, they are an application of the Scholastic theologians such as Thomas Aquinas or Robert Bellarmine. Contemporary papal teaching is an attempt to apply these valid metaphysical and moral principles to new problems that have arisen from the Enlightenment and the Industrial Revolution.

In this book, I undertake to give a new compendium of Catholic teachings concerning society. I have chosen a systematic approach both because this is more scientific and because it more clearly illustrates how the practical teachings of the Church of the last hundred years are derived from principles taught by both reason and revelation. In part 1, I will examine the nature of society and theoretical principles of the social order. I will then apply these to distinguish three basic human societies: the family, the State, and the Church. In part 2, I will apply theory to practice and enumerate a Catholic vision of how the most basic human societies, the family and the State, must pursue their goals. In accord with traditional Catholic thought, I will treat economics as an extension of the family, and also derive some practical points on business ethics.

This study is then offered to the reader to encourage him to participate in the development of a Christian view of the social order. As he applies what is examined here, he might keep in mind the *Epistle to Diognetus*, written by an unknown author sometime between AD 130 and the end of the second century.

> For the Christians are distinguished from other men neither by country, nor language, nor the customs which they observe. For they neither inhabit cities of their own, nor employ a peculiar form of speech, nor lead a life which is marked out by any singularity. The course of conduct which they follow has not been devised by any speculation or deliberation of inquisitive men; nor do they, like some, proclaim themselves the advocates of any merely human doctrines. But, inhabiting Greek as well as barbarian cities, according as the lot of each of them has determined, and following the customs of the natives in respect to clothing, food, and the rest of their ordinary conduct, they display to us their wonderful and confessedly striking method of life. They dwell in their own countries, but simply as sojourners. As citizens, they share in all things with others, and yet endure all things as if foreigners. Every foreign land is to them as their native country, and every land of their birth as a land of strangers. They marry, as do all [others]; they beget children; but they do not destroy their offspring. They have a common

table, but not a common bed. They are in the flesh, but they do not live after the flesh (2 Corinthians 10:3). They pass their days on earth, but they are citizens of heaven (Philippians 3:20). They obey the prescribed laws, and at the same time surpass the laws by their lives. They love all men, and are persecuted by all. They are unknown and condemned; they are put to death, and restored to life (2 Corinthians 6:9). They are poor, yet make many rich (2 Corinthians 6:10); they are in lack of all things, and yet abound in all; they are dishonored, and yet in their very dishonor are glorified. They are evil spoken of, and yet are justified; they are reviled, and bless (2 Corinthians 4:12); they are insulted, and repay the insult with honor; they do good, yet are punished as evil-doers. When punished, they rejoice as if quickened into life; they are assailed by the Jews as foreigners, and are persecuted by the Greeks; yet those who hate them are unable to assign any reason for their hatred.[2]

[2] *Epistle to Diognetus*, chap. 5.

⟶◈ PART 1 ◈⟵
Foundational Principles

ONE

Human Nature and Society

Origin and Method of the Study

Why does the Church discuss social questions? Does the Church have a social mission to solve political difficulties? The Second Vatican Council is explicit on this subject:

> The Church, by reason of her role and competence, is not identified with any political community nor bound by ties to any political system. It is at once the sign and the safeguard of the transcendental dimension of the human person. The political community and the Church are autonomous and independent of each other in their own fields. Nevertheless, both are devoted to the personal vocation of man, though under different titles.[3]

Thus the Church speaks about social matters in her competence to direct and guide the human person ethically. She tries to clarify what

[3] Vatican Council II, pastoral constitution *Gaudium et Spes* (December 7, 1965), no. 76.

is good or evil in social matters to inform Christians regarding their various rights and duties in the family and the State, the conformity of morality with human nature, and to judge problems and concerns that threaten the mission of the Church.

The Church does not have any specific political goal or direct any particular people as to what government they should choose. The Church can and does assert what sorts of governments and laws are just and unjust and bid the Christian to obedience in conscience. The Church can and does have the competence to define and assert solutions to problems concerning the State and family that are based in their character as human and ethical institutions. "Not that the Church has a mandate directly to regulate economic life. But the social and economic orders cannot be divorced from the moral, and it is her privilege and duty to affirm and proclaim the unchanging principles of morality."[4]

Each society — Church, State, and family — contributes something to the authentic development of the human person, and does this by the order which is fitting to attain this goal. One may not interfere with the other. The goals and order of the family and State are natural. The goal of the Church is supernatural: the vision of God in Heaven. It would be completely contrary to reason to use God as a means to a political end. Politics is the perfection of man's life in this world, which is limited and incomplete. God is infinite and cannot be an object of use, a means to any limited end.

The mission of the Church to define the nature of society and ethics is not one which depends solely on faith either to be known or to be explained. In the words of Pius XI:

> It is our right and duty to deal authoritatively with social
> and economic problems. It is not, of course, the office

---

[4]   Pius XII, *Address of July 16, 1947.*

of the Church to lead men to transient and perishable happiness only, but to that which is eternal; indeed the Church believes that it would be wrong for her to intervene without just cause in matters of earthly concern. But she never can relinquish her God-given task of interposing her authority not indeed in matters of technique, for which she has neither the equipment nor the competence, but in all those which fall under the moral law.[5]

There are several sources for this teaching. The first is the natural law and all the truths derived from it. This presupposes an objective human nature that is at one and the same time spiritual and material, a truth greatly questioned in modern theories of man. The second is Holy Scripture, which also teaches many salutary principles that accord with human reason. The third is the official Magisterium of the Church, which was instituted by Christ to authoritatively explain what is contained in Scripture and the Tradition of the Church. This includes papal encyclicals and conciliar documents. They decidedly are not the result of a common consensus among the faithful arrived at through a democratic vote on what social or moral teaching should be. The fourth source is human experience and science, because authentic philosophy presupposes ordinary common-sense experience.

As a result of the purpose and method of this study, Catholic social teaching is not one dimensional. It is characterized by a number of aspects. It is realistic because it seeks to express the nature and causes of human society considered in itself. This is in turn based on a realistic and objective metaphysics which recognizes the possibility of human

---

[5] Pius XI, encyclical letter *Quadragesimo Anno* (May 15, 1931), nos. 41–43.

knowledge arriving through sense experience at abstract concepts which truly express the realities known.

Catholic social teaching is also teleological. The nature of ethical actions in society is based on realizing the being-in-action of the nature of man. Societies are determined as to their order by what their final purpose is. Society must take account of the presence of God because He is the author of the natural law, which determines the perfection of man realized in societies. So social teaching is also theistic. "We approach the subject with confidence and in the exercise of our rights which manifestly pertain to us, for no practical solution to this question will be found apart from religion and the Church."[6] Finally, since Christ is the proper and efficacious means by which men return to the supernatural order through grace, social doctrine also must take into account the teaching of Christ.

Catholic social teaching is rooted in the Christian conception of man, and an examination of the theory of man is necessary to determine the proper goal and relationship of various societies. As this work is an exposition of Catholic thought on society, the fact that man has and can arrive at a supernatural goal at the end of his life is presumed. The Church always wants to make clear the unique character of man by teaching him the natural and supernatural means that dispose him to grace and that he uses to merit in the state of grace. These are not set aside in society, but in many cases, they are realized therein.

God: The Good of All Things

All Things Desire Their Final Unity in God

All things find their good in their last end. The final cause is the cause of causes. A being is composed to act in a certain way as a substance to attain its last end. All things that are composed find their source

---

[6] Leo XIII, encyclical letter *Rerum Novarum* (May 15, 1891), no. 13.

in unity and, as their end, desire to return to that unity which is the fount of their being. This end can only be found in the ultimate unity that is God, Who Himself is absolute unity. Since action follows being (*operari sequitur esse*), each thing attains its final unity according to its place in the order of being. This fact stretches from pure potential-to-be, which is called primary matter, to being itself, which has no potential. The whole universe of creatures manifests the potential to return from multiplicity to absolute unity in the highest degree. This absolute unity is perfect being, with no potential to be something else. It is not composed and so is absolutely one. In fact, it is God. All things act to return to the God from Whom they came. In this, they also "desire" to be like Him.

This order ascends as follows: pure potential, elements, mixed bodies, plants, animals, man, angels, God. Each level of this hierarchy can be said on its own level to "desire" to imitate God's goodness and unity. The first manifestation of this is seen in the fact that all things resist corruption and resist death. They are driven to subsist in themselves (for example, to be one, to be happy, to be good). This "desire" is only perfected in those creatures that have the ability to arrive at God by transcending matter, because only in God are action and being one and the same thing. In every other being, they are really distinct. In God, there is no potentiality. He is continuous act itself. All other beings have some mixture of act and potential, not fully realized unless they can rejoin God, from Whom they sprang.

This potentiality to exist in a further perfection is the source of motion. Mixed bodies, plants, and animals all exhibit this tendency. They seek to resemble God in their distinctive kind of activity. A stone seeks unity with the earth by the force of gravity. In a low-level sense, it can be said to "desire" to be like God in this motion. Plants seek this unity by growth and reproduction, when many elements are unified in organic being. Animals do the same by self-movement, passions, and sensitive joy. Their unity is even more prefect because they do not have to destroy the beings they experience through the senses in order to unify them in a sensitive way. Though all these beings desire unity with God as their perfect unity, such a unity as a result of movement can only be found in the spiritual order that arises from those beings that have an intellect and will. This is because they have a capacity to go beyond the order of matter and experience other beings in a spiritual way and, thus, union with God, Who is in essence not material.

Thus, one could say that from the pure potentiality-to-be to the pure act which is God, there are numerous intermediate existences showing different grades of being in different essences. The substance that is the human soul fulfills all the lower orders of material creation in their quest for unity. This is because the human soul is the means by which all the lower orders can arrive at the spiritual order. Man is a being composed of both a spiritual soul and flesh. The dignity of the human person becomes clear as the means by which spirit and matter come together and creation is able to attain its final purpose. God, Whose unity is the final good and perfection that all material things seek, becomes capable of attainment in and through the human soul. Since man substantially has a body, and this body is supported in existence and action by a human soul that is spiritual, the final perfection of creation is realized in and through human actions. This is very well expressed in a pagan author whom many Christian thinkers used to explain this: "Man stands on the horizon of being, between flesh and spirit, between time and eternity."[7]

Dignity of the Human Person

The dignity of man is based on the character of the human soul. Does the soul exist in its own right? In a sense, yes; in another sense, no.

---

[7] Proclus, *Liber de Causis.*

Two things are necessary for a thing to exist in its own right. It must subsist in itself. The human soul does. After the body dies, it continues to exist. It must also be a complete thing in itself as a nature. It should be able to be assigned a genus or species. This is not true of the human soul. The soul is not man. Man is a substantial unity of body and soul.

The source of the knowledge of the immortality of the soul is the observation, which even Aristotle made, that the soul has an act that transcends matter: intellection. This is the ability to know real, objective universal ideas through sense experience. The evolution which this knowledge caused in philosophical reflection on the world is essential to understanding the difference between a merely materialistic view of man and the Catholic idea of man.

The Pre-Socratics[8] denied both kinds of existence to the human soul. Empedocles, for example, maintained that the soul was a harmony of pure material elements. The understanding of the soul taught by the Pre-Socratics was basically one of exaggerated materialism. This is not because they rejected the spirit, but rather because they had not discovered it yet. Plato discovered the spirit, but then did not know what to do with matter. For him, it was an illusion. Thomas Aquinas remarks that it was not until Aristotle discovered the spiritual prime mover at the end of the study of the *Physics* that the human race advanced in a philosophical revolution to understand that the only way

---

[8] These are the Greek philosophers who lived before Plato and Aristotle. They are generally held to include Thales, Anaximander, Anaximenes, Pythagoras, Heraclitus, Parmenides, Empedocles, Anaxagoras, Democritus, and Leucippus. According to Aristotle in his *Metaphysics*, all these philosophers had one thing in common: they sought the ultimate causes through wonder at the effects of motion they experienced in the world. They discovered three of the classic four causes: material, final, and efficient. The formal cause eluded them, though, because until Socrates, no one discovered the substantial form and primary matter that transcends matter.

to completely explain physical motion was by arriving through sense experience at a mover who transcended matter.

The school that exaggerates the material nature of the human soul has a modern heir in a social philosophy like totalitarianism, which defines the only person as the collective state sometimes represented in the leader (*Duce, Führer*). Marxism also views the individual as absorbed in the collective, which is only a materialist conglomeration. Individuals in society would be mere appendages of the collective, whether it is of the fascist or Marxist variety.

The discovery and explanation of the human soul rests on the discovery of the act of intelligence and the accompanying truth to this, which is that willing represents a power that also transcends the order of matter. Neither act can be reduced to a material organ. The intellect cannot be reduced to the brain, and the will cannot be reduced to the physical heart or even the passions. If the soul has an act going beyond matter (knowledge and love), this presumes that, as a being, it must also go beyond this order. Such a non-material act requires a power which subsists in itself. Thus, the intellectual soul exercises its own act of existence as a subsisting thing. Indeed, it can perform such an act without the aid of the body. The soul can exist without the body, as happens after death. It is in intellection and willing that such an act is seen.

Yet, although this is true, it does not mean that the soul of man is a complete genus or species. Man is not a complete being without the body. Both the body and the soul are necessary for the existence of the substance man. Plato has this problem. Through examining the science of mathematics, Plato came to the conclusion that there was such a thing as knowledge of the non-material in man. Since he understood the act of the soul that caused this also to be non-material, he asserted that the soul of man was his species. For him, the relation of the soul to the body in man is accidental. The soul uses the body as a ship, and the body has an imprisoning character. Because of his theory of disembodied forms, Plato posited that there were several souls in man, each corresponding to the kinds of acts he saw human beings perform. There was one soul in man corresponding to his spiritual acts, another to his sensitive acts, and another to his organic acts. Just as there were many sailors in one ship — a captain, a mate, a cook, and so on — so there were many souls in one body. There was only a tenuous relation of the soul to the body, and the best way to experience knowledge was to deny the senses altogether.

Even Christian thought influenced by Plato has never accepted this point of view. Though the works of Aristotle were little-known in the Church until the Crusades, Christian thought has always treated the soul as Aristotle explained it: the form of the body in substantial union with it. This is also the scriptural point of view. Some contemporary authors have made much of the fact there are no words in Hebrew that correspond to an exact distinction between the soul and the body. They have posited that one cannot reconcile Greek thought with Scripture. One must remember there was no one Greek theory concerning the union of the soul with the body, and though Christian thought has generally accepted as dogma that the soul can exist without the body, it has never gone so far as to say that the body is not man. Quite the opposite. "The unity of soul and body is so profound that one has to consider the soul to be the 'form' of the body:[9] i.e., it is because of its spiritual soul that the body made of matter becomes a living, human body; spirit and matter, in man, are not two natures united, but rather their union forms a single nature" (*CCC* 365). The idea that there is a hard and fast separation of the soul from the body has more in common with Plato than with Aristotle. Aristotle's concept of the union

---

[9] Council of Vienne (1312): DS 902.

of the soul and body has much more in common with Hebrew and Christian ideas on the subject than Plato's.

The Church has always declared that the soul in man is one that is in substantial union with the body and underlies all of the activities that man performs, including those of the body. The soul gives the body a real existence, and the physical functions of the body testify to that. There is a difference in being between a human eye found in a dead body and a living one. The eye of a dead man is only a human eye in a certain respect, because it lacks the animating principle of the soul. So though it has all the powers necessary for sight physically, such an action cannot be performed by a dead man. The soul is something that can subsist in itself, but nonetheless, it is connected to a body to make a complete being found in the species man, a rational animal. This is why until the general resurrection, there is a lack of nature in man. The soul may be completely happy seeing God, but without the body, "man" does not see God. "The desire of the separated soul is entirely at rest, as regards the thing desired; since, to wit, it has that which suffices its appetite. But it is not wholly at rest, as regards the desirer, since it does not possess that good in every way that it would wish to possess it. Consequently, after the body has been resumed, happiness increases not in intensity, but in extent (*non intensive sed extensive*)."[10]

What kind of existence does the soul have? Every form shares something in the operation proper to forms that are both above it and below it in the order of being. For example, motion in animals shares the lower form of growth and nutrition characteristic of organisms like plants, but it also has a kind of anticipation of intelligence in man through the ability the animal has to know a good sensibly and move itself to possess it. The dog knows and desires food, for example. The lamb sees a wolf and runs away. This can be quite extensive and

---

[10] Thomas Aquinas, *Summa Theologica*, I–II, q. 4, art. 5, ad. 5.

sophisticated through instinct. Aristotle was so impressed by this fact that he held there was a kind of prudence in animals. But animals do not have intellectual knowledge or desire, despite this sophisticated presence in them of instinct, because they cannot abstract to real, objective universal ideas.

In a similar way, the human soul shares something with the lower orders of creation in that it exhibits all the characteristics of both organic and sensible life. Man also participates in the pure intellectual knowledge found in God and the angels, though not in such a deep sense. Man abstracts through the senses, which he shares with the animals, but he is not deeply and instantaneously intelligent, as is the case with the angels and God. He finds metaphysics very hard and tiring.

Thus man summarizes in his person two activities: (1) he has a resemblance to the angels because he shows intellectual knowledge and love (Spiritual Order) and (2) he differs from the angels in that he exercises this spiritual knowledge and love through his sense and emotional life (Material Order). In his spiritual self, he touches Heaven, and in his material self, he lifts up the earth. Man, in his nature, can truly be said to stand in the middle of creation between flesh and spirit, between time and eternity.

Thomas Aquinas reflects this twofold aspect of human nature when he says:

> For one thing to be another's substantial form, two requirements must be met. First, the form must be the principle of the substantial being of the thing whose form it is; I speak not of the productive but of the formal principle whereby a thing exists and is called a being. The second requirement then follows from this, namely, that the form and the matter be joined together in the unity of one act of being; which is not true of the union

of the efficient cause with that to which it gives being. And this single act of being is that in which the composite substance subsists: a thing one in being and made up of matter and form. Now, as we have shown, the fact that an intellectual substance is subsistent does not stand in the way of its being the formal principle of the being of the matter, as communicating its own being to the matter. For it is not unfitting that the composite and its form should subsist in the same act of being, since the composite exists only by the form, and neither of them subsists apart from the other.[11]

In the unity of the soul, there are two complimentary orders of being. This is not duality in action. Although there are three levels of action in man — (1) self-movement like the plants, (2) sense knowledge like the animals, and (3) intellect and will like the angels — there are not several souls in man as Plato thought. St. Thomas teaches that the soul is substantially one, organic, sensitive, and intellectual, and is immediately united with the body in the material order. However, the proper activity of the soul, which sets the human being apart from the

---

[11] "Quod aliquid sit forma substantialis alterius, duo requiruntur. Quorum unum est, ut forma sit principium essendi substantialiter ei cuius est forma: principium autem dico, non factivum, sed formale, quo aliquid est et denominatur ens. Unde sequitur aliud, scilicet quod forma et materia conveniant in uno esse: quod non contingit de principio effectivo cum eo cui dat esse. Et hoc esse est in quo subsistit substantia composita, quae est una secundum esse, ex materia et forma constans. Non autem impeditur substantia intellectualis, per hoc quod est subsistens, ut probatum est, esse formale principium essendi materiae, quasi esse suum communicans materiae. Non est enim inconveniens quod idem sit esse in quo subsistit compositum et forma ipsa: cum compositum non sit nisi per formam, nec seorsum utrumque subsistat." Thomas Aquinas, *Summa Contra Gentiles*, II, q. 68.

rest of creation, is understanding, and the soul is able to understand without a bodily organ since it subsists in itself.

There are important implications for society in this twofold character of the soul. Many have thought that it was only the state of sin that made society necessary for human fulfillment. The necessity of society called the social character, or solidarity in more contemporary writers, is actually founded on the rational character of this human soul. It is a moral union of wills formed by many individuals acting through choice together to pursue some reasoning good that each could not attain if left to himself. Bees, though they have order and act together, have no society because they have no choice and reasoning direction. Human society, rather, is caused by a number of people acting together to realize goods of the soul on various levels of human nature. By intellectual knowledge, these people can know the nature of these goods and also how to evaluate the means necessary to attain them. Since man touches both the material and spiritual orders, these actions and the order important for them have both material and spiritual characters. The final realization of this good is in the communion of saints that characterizes the society in which the Church is finally perfect, the Beatific Vision of Heaven.

Man and Society

Man, therefore, is a rational animal composed of body and soul. The final goal of this being is God Himself, and this union with God is realized in the Mystical Body of Christ, the society of the Church, that society by which people arrive at the Beatific Vision. "Man has a spiritual and immortal soul. He is a person, marvelously endowed by his Creator with gifts of body and mind. He is a true 'microcosm' as the ancients said, a world in miniature with a value far surpassing that of the vast and inanimate cosmos. God alone is his last end, in this life and in the next. By sanctifying grace he is raised to the dignity of a son of God, and incorporated into the Kingdom of God in the Mystical Body of Christ."[12]

In his inner constitution, the human person differs from all the rest of material creation. The real greatness of man lies in his immortal and spiritual soul, by which he can have a special relationship with God. The dignity of man consists in those actions that befit this soul. This means that man cannot finally be perfected by any action that he can attain by his own power in this life. Actions that are within the reach of human power are necessary in this life because the body is a natural component of man. This is the purpose of the political and domestic good. Though these goods are necessary to man, they can never exhaust the potential present in the human soul to know truth. Marxism and totalitarianism tend to reduce man to a mere appendage of matter at worst and the body politic at best. In these political philosophies, the body politic is viewed as though it were a person, but the individuals who make it up are not.

Created things tend to their goal, which is God, by acts proper to their own natures. Material things do this by imitation, and so they are often called the footprints (*vestigia*) of God. Man, however, is made in the image and likeness of God Himself, and thus every human person can have a direct relationship with God and can be directly governed by Him. The reasoning creature has the ability to know the divine plan and to participate in fully and completely realizing that plan by cooperating with God's plan. As a result, John Paul II calls man a "partner with the Absolute."[13]

Some other definitions of man popular in modern philosophy are a being with a history (*homo historicus*) or a being who works (*homo*

---

[12] Pius XI, encyclical letter *Divini Redemptoris* (March 19, 1937), no. 27.
[13] John Paul II, *Male and Female He Created Them* (Boston: Pauline Books and Media, 2006), 151.

factor). None of these does justice to complete human fulfillment. Man is *homo viator*, a pilgrim and wayfarer on a journey to a final fulfillment he cannot find in this life.

The human soul is of such a character that it permeates the whole of man. The whole man experiences something, not just the eye or the heart or the foot or the brain. Man has a special place in providence because he stands above other creatures as to their nature and their final purpose. In nature, only the creature with reason has dominion over his own actions and thus can claim responsibility. He can freely move himself or simply not move himself. The dignity of his final purpose is witnessed by the fact that only a being with an intellect and will can universalize and act beyond material determination to arrive at the final end of the world by knowing and loving. Other beings attain their end by participation in simply being, like God. Man attains his end by image and likeness in knowledge and love, and so there is one way by which reasoning creatures arrive at their destination and another by which unreasoning creatures arrive at the same destination. Only reasoning creatures can actually arrive at God, and thus, though being like God is the end of everything, only man can be said to arrive at this goal and so rest happy in God.

Because they transcend matter in both being and acting for a goal, reasoning beings cannot be reduced to mere material things for manipulation. Instead, they are governed for their own sakes. Pope John Paul II expresses the twofold aspect of this very well: "The first affirms that man is the only creature in the world that the Creator willed 'for his own sake;' the second consists in saying that this same man, willed in this way by the Creator from the 'beginning,' can only find himself through a disinterested gift of self."[14] The very kind of being man is requires God's personal, providential care. Other things are subordinated

[14] John Paul II, General Audience (January 16, 1980).

to him as a kind of instrument. They are only useful for another being. Man is a principal agent. He holds dominion over his acts and so is free in his activity, not a slave who is only useful as a tool for someone or something else. The reasoning creature is the only one free by nature. Things that are ordered to an end by another cannot attain that end by their own power. Instead, they are subordinated to those things that do attain the end. Only one with an intellectual nature can attain God in Himself by knowing and loving Him. Angels and men are the only beings absolutely required for the ultimate perfection of the universe. All other material things are subject to them.

Of all the things that exist, angels and men are closest to God in knowledge and love. The intellect allows these beings to comprehend the whole of existing things, whereas others only have their share in existence. God provides in a special way a stewardship over creation for angels and men. Since man has a body, this implies an important stewardship over material things. This does not mean that he can use them as he pleases for any purpose. They can only be used for the purpose that God has in providing them, and this is governed by the moral law.

Everything that exists realizes its perfection in action. Each thing is ordered to act in the manner in which it is subordinated to God because, as the absolute unity, each seeks to return to Him. Angels and men receive direction from God not only as to the kind of act that must be done but also as to how these acts perfect the individual. Since men are governed for their own sakes, they are governed as individuals and not just as members of a collective or herd. Human beings must morally participate in this government. Natural inclinations are not enough for the perfection of human acts, as they are in plants and animals. Men must also direct their acts interiorly and individually by the use of their free will. God created individual creatures of such a kind that He knew they were suited to attain the end under His governance. Only men, as a species and individually, have the capacity under His governance to direct themselves in being able to grasp how these actions contribute to this perfection or deny it, how they are good or evil. In this way, men can know divine providence and participate in it. They thus exercise dominion in things though a participated dominion, not an absolute one. By doing this, they can govern their own actions and even those of others.

The dignity of man consists in the crowning of his free acts in perpetual existence not only on the level of species, as is the case with other things with the passage of life and death, but also on the level of the individual. Dogs beget dogs and so the species goes on despite death. But men go on also as individuals. They live forever.

Man is an independent being with a spiritual nature. The spiritual nature of man is the source of his dignity and also of his freedom. The human person is unique, and his individuality is given to him through the union of his body with the soul that informs it. The one and the same human is a person whether viewed from the side of the spirit or viewed from the side of matter. The soul, then, is a substance that is non-materially subsistent and so is a person. As a species, it must exist in composition with the body, which is the basis for its individuality.

Thus, the only society whose final cause fully perfects man as a person through the spiritual and supernatural order is the Church. This is why the Church transcends the political order, because though the political order can play a role in perfecting the person, it cannot do so completely by offering truth and love as such. The State and the family perfect man as a person from the side of his corporeal nature. They also contribute to his spiritual perfection, but cannot lead him to that final act where he is completely perfect in God.

> Man is not ordered to the political community according to his whole self and all which is his. Thus it is not

necessary that each act be meritorious or demeritorious through order to the political community. But the whole which is man, and which he can do and has, must be ordered to God. Thus every good or evil act of man has an essential element of merit or demerit respecting God, as far as it is from the essential element of act.[15]

Since the human person has many levels of perfection, one must examine which level of man is perfected in which society. The primary goal of man is to develop the spiritual self. Each society develops the spiritual self in its own way by realizing it in act. The distinction of the human soul between person (subsistent spiritual being) and individual (single being with a material nature) only has meaning if interpreted to be the same man looked at from different points of view. The dignity of man demands he always act in conformity with his spiritual nature, even if the actions are very sensual and material.

There are, therefore, a number of obligations that flow from this spiritual dignity. Man must pursue his final purpose in such a way that he can actually arrive at it. This requires that his pursuit of this good be carried out by means of virtuous actions. These virtuous actions not only respect God and His inner nature, but also include moral virtues that are developed in the temporal order of this world. Indeed, though man is made for Heaven, he arrives at this goal through his pilgrimage here on earth.

---

[15] "Homo non ordinatur ad communitatem politicam secundum se totum, et secundum omnia sua, et ideo non oportet quod quilibet actus eius sit meritorius vel demeritorius per ordinem ad communitatem politicam. Sed totum quod homo est, et quod potest et habet, ordinandum est ad Deum, et ideo omnis actus hominis bonus vel malus habet rationem meriti vel demeriti apud Deum, quantum est ex ipsa ratione actus." Aquinas, *Summa Theologica*, I–II, q. 21, art. 4, ad. 3.

When man truly wills some good, that willed act naturally enters into the external order as an imperated act, if this is required, unless inhibited by something that is outside his power to control. The human person must act freely. His responsibility and thus interior formation is determined by the freedom of his actions. The root of that freedom is in the will, but the cause of that freedom is in the intellect.[16] Thus, the person is both qualified and obliged to take responsibility for his actions. To do this, he must remain inwardly free and must refuse to carry out the orders of authority when these conflict a right, certain, and informed conscience.

Before we examine further the significance of freedom, we have to emphasize that this inner independence of ego in relation of the intentional objects of volition (i.e. the value-end) is justified by self-reliance. Thus any interpretation of free will, if it is to conform to reality, must rely on man's auto determinism instead of floating in the air by stressing indeterminism. It is clearly visible in the structure of experience that in the interpretation of the functional aspect of freedom indeterminism assumes a secondary role while auto determinism has a primary and fundamental importance.[17]

This freedom—the specific independence from objects in the intentional order, the ability to choose among them, to decide about them—does not, however, abolish the fact that man is conditioned in the broadest sense by the world of objects, in particular, by

[16] "Radix libertatis est voluntas sicut subiectum, sed sicut causa, est ratio." Aquinas, *Summa Theologica*, I–II, q. 17, art. 1, ad. 2.

[17] Karol Wojtyła, *The Acting Person* (Boston: D. Reidel Publishing Company, 1979), 121.

the domain of values. For his is not the freedom from objects and values, but on the contrary, the freedom of, or rather for objects or values.[18]

This understanding of the origin of the person is by no means the only one, and since it is crucial to determining the place of man in society, the modern ones must be considered.

Liberal Capitalism

One major school of thought on the origin of the person very important to understanding modern social problems is the school of liberal capitalism. This cannot be understood unless viewed in relation to the economic and Industrial Revolution in the late eighteenth and early nineteenth centuries. The prime developers of this school are Adam Smith (1723–1790) and David Ricardo (1772–1823). Their aim was to provide economic stimulus to business in reaction to the excessive state protectionism of mercantilism. The reaction to excessive state control was the exaltation of the individual freed from all exterior control. This was coupled with a development in Enlightenment ideas which reacted to the problem of evil, confronting the best-of-all-possible-worlds motif.

The rationalists of the seventeenth century had basically held that the natural laws had come so perfect from the hands of the divine watchmaker that this was the best of all possible worlds and could not be any better. People such as Voltaire in *Candide* demonstrated that this was an impossible position, as it failed to take account of evil. The theory was then modified so that there were perfect laws that governed the world in a deterministic way, but these came about in an evolutionary pattern so that change was always for the best. The potential for perfection was in

---

[18] Ibid., 132.

the mechanism, which was not perfect yet, but progress would make it perfect if human beings just did not interfere with this evolution. Human beings had to simply discover what these laws were and how to use the mechanism to accommodate themselves to this materialistic progress, and all would become naturally more perfect.

In economics, this resulted in a theory in which all outside influence on the market was alien to economic progress. The law of supply and demand was absolute, and no one, especially the State, could interfere with this law. This theory led to several problematic elements.

The first was a loss of ethics in business. These theorists emphasized the absolute autonomy of human activities in relation to the objective order of man. One who understands the law of supply and demand must be freed from all objective bases outside of this law. The economy becomes completely determined by the will of the individual who can discern this, and this is totally distinct from ethics. Making money and the human good are equated. As long as the business is prospering, it does not matter if the product is good or the service is well provided, except as an issue of profit. It makes no sense, therefore, to speak of justice or injustice when it comes to the economic order. Property is the norm for each man, and the individual developing his property according to the fixed deterministic laws of the marketplace is the standard or norm on which all economic justice is based. As a result, he becomes a law unto himself.

A corollary to this principle is the exaltation of competition. This takes place in three ways. First, there is the historic fact of overcoming state protectionism, the controls on commerce that held economic competition back in the past, such as the craft guilds and mercantilism. These controls are useless and harmful because they fail to recognize the law of material progress. They are not unjust, just anachronistic. Second, there must be a change from cottage industries to mass production. This is necessary to stimulate supply and demand. Third, the boundless optimism that change is always for the best and progress by free enterprise always produces prosperity must be guaranteed by no outside interference, especially by state laws. The free interplay between mass production and supply and demand will naturally produce economic prosperity. The product is more important than the person who made it or the person for whom it is destined.

The extreme application of these principles leads to the complete absence of the State from any regulation at all of the economic order (also known as *laissez-faire*). Any authority of the State regarding economic affairs is useless, harmful, and unjust. It is considered useless because of the absolute evolutionary mechanism in the laws of economy. It is harmful because it frustrates the complete freedom of the individual in self-realization. It is not just because justice demands the complete, unfettered freedom of the subject. The liberal states faithfully implemented this stance without criticism throughout the nineteenth century.

The last implementation of this philosophy was the absolute exaltation of the freedom of the individual. The order of subjective freedom was emphasized to the complete denial of the objective order. Though it is true that man has a right to private property, the subjectivism and abstract emphasis on progress and the autonomy of reason led to the denial of the balance provided by the affirmation of the social aspect of property.

In civil law, judges based their standard for justice on the absolute freedom of the private contract, no matter how unjust toward the worker. The State could not nullify private contracts, and collective contracts were forbidden. Le Chapelier, for example, opined in 1791: "There are no longer State corporations, there is only the individual interest of each one and the general interest of all. It belongs to free individual convention to fix the working day for every worker and it belongs to each workman to maintain the contract fixed with the one who employs him."

This economic theory tends to reduce the rights of the worker to a mere function of the law of supply and demand and mass production.

Man is no longer the subject of work, but merely one machine among others. The popes condemned this Enlightenment theory because it failed to do justice to the fact that economics was created by man and for man, and that work should always have a human dimension. One can find this condemnation of errors listed in such a document as the *Syllabus of Errors*:

> 56. Moral laws do not stand in need of the divine sanction, and it is not at all necessary that human laws should be made conformable to the laws of nature and receive their power of binding from God. — Allocution "Maxima quidem," June 9, 1862.
>
> 57. The science of philosophical things and morals and also civil laws may and ought to keep aloof from divine and ecclesiastical authority. — Ibid.
>
> 58. No other forces are to be recognized except those which reside in matter, and all the rectitude and excellence of morality ought to be placed in the accumulation and increase of riches by every possible means, and the gratification of pleasure. — Ibid.; Encyclical "Quanto conficiamur," Aug. 10, 1863.
>
> 59. Right consists in the material fact. All human duties are an empty word, and all human facts have the force of right. — Allocution "Maxima quidem," June 9, 1862.
>
> 60. Authority is nothing else but numbers and the sum total of material forces. — Ibid.
>
> 61. The injustice of an act when successful inflicts no injury on the sanctity of right. — Allocution "Jamdudum cernimus," March 18, 1861.

62. The principle of non-intervention, as it is called, ought to be proclaimed and observed. — Allocution "Novos et ante," Sept. 28, 1860.[19]

Marxism

The exact opposite of this theory is that of Karl Marx. According to Marx, the emphasis on human individuality was created by the material determinism of history. The human person develops historically, economically, and politically by deterministic necessity. This development is from community to trade to individual capital to world individualism.

For Marx, there are no ethics, no right and wrong, justice or injustice in capitalism. Capitalism is one stage in those natural laws that matter and its development obey. The competition of capitalism and the destruction of state protectionism was a necessary stage in the development of mass production that allowed for world materialism. Matter was compared to a baby with clothes. The clothes were the function of the development of matter, which included justice, truth, and religion. As matter grows through the necessity of evolution, the clothes begin to constrict the baby. The violent class revolution is the ripping asunder of the baby clothes to make room for a more advanced stage in the development of matter. The social structure that creates the middle class and emphasized private property and competition naturally develops into the classless society characterized by the world individual. Capitalism and the bourgeois society are not unjust; they are simply outdated. The person created by capitalism must now be transcended to allow for the universal development of matter.

[19] Pius IX, *Syllabus of Errors* (December 8, 1864).

Marx says:

> Man is isolated only through the historical process.
> Originally, he is introduced as a *generic tribal essence*, a
> dependent animal. Trade itself is one of the principal
> means of his isolation. It renders superfluous depen-
> dency and rescinds it.[20]

The cooperation in the process of labor which we
find predominately at the beginning of the civilizing of
humanity with hunters, for example, in the community
of agriculture of the Indians, rests on the one hand on
the common ownership of production, on the other
hand, on the fact that the individual has not yet cut the
umbilical cord of the tribe or of the community as the
single bee does not grow tired of the hive.[21]

In this society of free competition, the individual
appears untied from natural bonds, etc. that in the pre-
ceding period of time made him an accessory part of the
human collectivity, determined and circumscribed. The
period of history that generates this way of looking at
things that of the isolated individual is on the contrary
the epoch of more developed social relations.[22]

The bourgeoisie have had a great revolutionary
function in history, when joined to power. They have
destroyed all the conditions of feudal, patriarchal, and
romantic life. They have cut without reverence the mul-
ticolored bonds which in feudal society bound man to
his natural superiors, but have not cut between man

[20] Karl Marx, *Lineamenti*, vol. II, 173.
[21] Karl Marx, *Capital*, I, 375–76.
[22] Karl Marx, *Introduction of 1857*, 3.

and man without chains, that of naked advantage, the ruthless payment of cash.[23]

True Origin and Characteristics of the Human Person

Since the human person is a being ordered to God, civil society can perfect him, but not in any final sense. As a composite of body and soul, the final act that perfects his being must be fulfillment in God by vision of Him. The value of the person is seen in his enjoyment of God. Grace is the means toward that enjoyment, and so one single person in the state of grace transcends the material good of the whole universe. "Justification is the *most excellent work of God's love* made manifest in Christ Jesus and granted by the Holy Spirit. It is the opinion of St. Augustine that 'the justification of the wicked is a greater work than the creation of heaven and earth,' because 'heaven and earth will pass away but the salvation and justification of the elect ... will not pass away.' He holds also that the justification of sinners surpasses the creation of the angels in justice, in that it bears witness to a greater mercy" (CCC 1994).

The intense spiritual life required for this is far greater than all other activities of man. This life of grace is implemented in the Church. It surpasses other human works since grace does not destroy but perfects nature; yet the Church is not alien to or against other human societies. Rather, the Church affirms that some of those other societies — namely, the family and the State — are necessary for the perfection of the good of the person in this world.

Thomas Aquinas holds that "the person signifies what is most perfect in all nature, namely a subsistent being with a rational nature."[24]

---

[23] Ibid., 4.

[24] "Persona significant id quod est perfectissimum in tota natura, scilicet subsistens in rationali natura." Aquinas, *Summa Theologica*, I, q. 29, art. 3.

Though in his *Summa* this definition applies primarily to God, it is also used with appropriate changes respecting the human person. It is clear from this definition that to be rational is one of the specifying characteristics of being a person and the source of dignity. This makes the person a unique being, who has at one and the same time a subsistent rational and material nature, as has already been discussed.

In metaphysics, the term *subsistent subject,* or *suppositum,* is reserved to designate a concrete being with all its perfections. The being in its principal and proper sense is a *suppositum.* A subsistent being is not just form or matter, or substance without accidents, or a being distinct from its essence, but includes the whole resulting union of all these elements. The properties of subsistent being are based on this unique individuality, which, in the final analysis, is incommunicable with any other being. These are individuality, subsistence, and incommunicability.

Only singular things really exist. There is no such thing as a universal essence that is a subsistent subject. The universal could not receive the act of being in itself, but only in the individual thing.

Not every individual thing is a subsistent being. Accidents are individual, but they do not exist in and of themselves. The same is true of the material components of a substance, such as the heart and the foot. Only the individual substance exists in its own right. In a rational subsistent being, the individual is the same as the person.

As a result of this subsistence, the subject cannot be interchanged or communicated with another. While a property or an accident can be communicated in many subjects, the individual is something unique and so distinct from other things that there is no possibility that those other things can participate in it. There may be a relationship between subsistent beings, but not direct participation.

As a result, a person is distinctly found only in reasoning beings. Since human and angelic persons have a reasoning nature, they possess by nature a similarity to the ultimate Persons, the Divine Persons of the Trinity Who demonstrate both incommunicability and society in the supreme form. The most fitting relationship between these Persons, because of their reasoning nature, is truth and love. The personalistic norm of Vatican II, already invoked, expresses this truth: "The first affirms that man is the only creature in the world that the Creator willed 'for his own sake;' the second consists in saying that this same man, willed in this way by the Creator from the 'beginning,' can only find himself through a disinterested gift of self."[25] Catholicism has always argued against Manichaeism in all its forms, proclaiming the goodness of the body and matter. However, it would be morally evil to proclaim that matter was the exclusive or even the most important human good. In fact, the essence of sin consists in the conversion to changeable or created good and aversion from unchangeable good, which is God. This, again, is not to say in any sense that created goods are not real goods in themselves. They become apparent goods when they rival or lead to a denial of God. In the same way, material goods are real human goods but become apparent when they rival or lead to a denial of spiritual goods. The individual cannot be sacrificed to the person, nor the person to the individual.

The Person in Man's Society (The Common Good)

What Fulfills the Person?

The personalistic norm evoked in Vatican II states that a person can only realize themselves fully in a disinterested gift of self to others. Social union is therefore necessary by nature for each person to finally realize the potential present in his spiritual nature. The necessity of this social union is especially true for those essential goods for the spiritual formation of the person. In terms of this world, this would

[25] John Paul II, General Audience (January 16, 1980).

be the family and the civil society. In terms of the next world, it would be the Church.

Society is a union of wills pursuing these goods, which are generally known as the "common good." This term is greatly misunderstood. For utilitarians and materialists, it has been defined as the greatest good for the greatest number of the sum of all the private goods of the members of the society. Actually, the common good is the experience of some perfection that a human person could not attain if left alone. The common good "is not simply the sum total of particular interests; rather it involves an assessment and integration of those interests on the basis of a balanced hierarchy of values."[26] The ability to experience family, marriage, and children is one such good. Commerce and the material prosperity necessary to support a family is another. Civil peace and order necessary to pursue justice, family life, and business is another. In other words, the spiritual nature of man must recognize that there is a metaphysical basis for the common good that alone can bring all the potentials present in the dignity of the human person into action. These potentials are both physical and spiritual. However, earthly society can never finally realize all the potentials present in man because only God is a pure Person, a complete totality.

Man, for example, can be partially fulfilled in the civil community, but never ultimately fulfilled. The domestic and civil community may dispose him to this fulfillment, but there only the final knowledge of God can complete the potential in the intellect for truth.

Since the nature of a society is determined by the goal in relation of the objective perfection of the person, one can say that only that society that offers the supernatural goal to man and an order that makes this possible of attainment is the true universal human society. This is the Church. This is at the basis of Thomas Aquinas's comment that all men

[26] John Paul II, encyclical letter *Centesimus Annus* (May 1, 1991), no. 47.

are either actually or potentially members of the Church except the damned.[27] This fact is perhaps also at the base of the rather surprising claim of Boniface VIII that all human beings are subject to the pope. This is not as a temporal ruler, but rather as a recognition that the servant of Christ on earth is the pope, who is the authority on earth for the sacramental order by which human beings can experience grace.

Vatican II took up the question of the salvation of those who were not Christians by saying that they were related to the Church. "Finally those who have not yet received the Gospel are related to the people of God in various ways."[28] Some have taken that to mean that one does not need to be a member of the Church to be saved. The council attached a note to that particular sentence that refers to the *Summa Theologica* of Thomas Aquinas where he states: "Those who are unbaptized, though not actually in the Church, are in the Church potentially. And this potentiality is rooted in two things — first and principally, in the power of Christ, which is sufficient for the salvation of the whole human race; secondly, in free-will."[29] Metaphysically, the person can only be fulfilled in the vision of God. Thus, the society that has the vision of God as its common good is the society that belongs properly and perpetually to all men.

The family and the civil order, however, perfect social goods in the societies that man can attain by his own natural power. Each directs the practical judgment of their members by laws or customs to perfect

---

[27] Aquinas, *Summa Theologica*, III, q. 8, art. 3, ad corp.

[28] Vatican Council II, Dogmatic Constitution on the Church *Lumen Gentium* (November 21, 1964), no. 16.

[29] "Dicendum quod illi qui sunt infideles, etsi actu non sint de Ecclesia, sunt tamen in potentia. Quae quidem potentia in duobus fundatur, primo quidem et principaliter, in virtute Christi, quae sufficiens est ad salutem totius humani generis; secundario, in arbitrii libertate." Aquinas, *Summa Theologica*, III, q. 8, art. 3, ad. 1.

some human potential on some level. The natural law deals with the person himself. The civil law and the family receive their power to bind the conscience from the fact that they implement the natural law, which is man's participation in the eternal law present in the mind of God. Any law that is not so directed but commands some action contrary to these laws cannot fulfill the person. Therefore, they are not true laws and so cannot bind the members of the society to obedience.

Modern theories of society do not recognize the common good because they do not recognize the transcendent quality of the person. Thus, they exalt the material side to the expense of the spiritual side and are anti-personal. This would be the case in liberal capitalism, where the only law is the individual human reason and so the private good formed by some sort of collective decision. There is no true common action in these societies or common work that realizes something beyond the good of the individual. Or these societies affirm the transcendent action of the group at the expense of the individual and are anti-individualistic, like Marxism or totalitarianism, where the individual is sacrificed to a materialist world order that is determined by something that does not recognize the spiritual nature of the person, such as class or race. There is a third problem with these societies, in that they often also destroy both the person and the individual by instituting some form of master person, like a duce, a führer, a leader, or even the collective, whose function is merely to organize the material individuals.

The Final Good of the Person

To understand the correct interpretation of the origin of the social character of the person, it is necessary to understand the difference between the Scholastic terms *being* and *act*. These are known in Scholastic philosophy as first and second act. First act is the essence of a being, or what it is. This may be a physical or spiritual form. It is the source of the qualitative character of the actions of the being that proceed from the kind of nature it possesses. Dogs act like dogs, leaves like leaves, and human beings like human beings. The maxim that governs this fact of nature is "*operari sequitur esse*" (action follows being).

First act is the ontological constitution of the thing. In man's case, this is the soul and the body with the powers that are characteristic of the kind of being they possess. So far, this has been the aspect of man that has been discussed in this book. Corresponding to this is the second act, which realizes or completes the powers present in first act, but in further potential to participate in being. The intellect, which can know truth, actually knows a truth; the will, which can love good, actually loves; the passions, which are drawn to various experiences, actually do love, hate, desire, and enjoy; the eye actually sees, and so forth. This latter experience is necessary to complete the human potential present in the ontological character of man. The only being that is not divided into first and second act and has no potentials that need to be further realized for perfection is God.

There are many further experiences in existence realized in act for human beings because of all the various potentials present in the human soul. What is the only object that can completely perfect these powers? This object would have to completely reduce these powers to act so there is no further perfection required. Many people have attempted to find this completion in many objects. This enjoyment of this object would also be identified with the happiness of man ethically.

An excellent discussion of the ability of various objects to realize human potential is found in both *The Consolation of Philosophy*, by Boethius, and the *Summa Contra Gentiles* (III, art. 25–63) of Thomas Aquinas. Both of these discussions place the final object of perfection outside the material order. St. Augustine recounts an equally instructive discussion concerning a survey of the "man on the street" of his time as to what this final perfection could consist in. In the *City of God*, he says: "And although they erred in a variety of ways, yet natural insight has prevented them from wandering from the truth so far that they have not placed the supreme good and evil, some in the soul, some in the body, and some in both. From this tripartite distribution of the sects of philosophy, Marcus Varro, in his book *De Philosophia*, has drawn so large a variety of opinions, that, by a subtle and minute analysis of distinctions, he numbers without difficulty as many as 288 sects, not that these have actually existed, but sects which are possible."[30] All of these opinions about the ultimate good were wrong.

Many place their happiness in the carnal pleasures of sex and the table. The difficulty with this opinion is that pleasure is a byproduct of another good. If one is thirsty, it is pleasant to drink, but tasting the water is the good as such that causes the pleasant and joyful sensation, and so it would be the object, not the pleasure. The pleasure is not sought for its own sake. Pleasure is something accompanying the good, not the good itself.

As to the pleasures of the table, there is always an evil side to sensible pleasures. The more you eat, the more you get fat; eventually, you are stuffed and then the food is undesirable.

Some look for their final object in honor or glory, but these cannot be the true place where happiness resides. They are merely recognitions of another good. They are often mistakenly given and, in themselves, have nothing to do with the satisfaction of the soul. Power is the ability to do something and is only as effective in satisfying human desire as the good that such power can bring. Aristotle thought that man most powerful who could control himself.

The same difficulty appears in all attempts to root the good in bodily goods. None of them can realize the soul as such, good and evil men possess them, they are often kept to the hurt of their owner, and the

---

[30] Augustine, *City of God*, bk. XIX, 1.

possessor has no control over them. Wealth can be lost in one economic collapse or one natural disaster.

Thomas Aquinas said that all men look to the future for good because they are not fully realized by anything in this world. This constant looking to the future is the recognition that there is no human experience of a sensible character that gives the final realization of man in second act to fulfill the highest and deepest powers of man. In both Aristotle and St. Thomas, the highest human activity is proclaimed to be an activity of the spiritual soul, which is the contemplation of divine truth. This activity alone satisfies the power of the intellect to enter into perfect act. The contemplation of truth is sought for its own sake and does not depend on any exterior cause to be attained or lost.

> If happiness is activity in accordance with virtue, it is reasonable that it should be in accordance with the highest virtue; and this will be that of the best thing in us. Whether it be reason or something else that is this element which is thought to be our natural ruler and guide and to take thought of things noble and divine, whether it be itself also divine or only the most divine element in us, the activity of this in accordance with its proper virtue will be perfect happiness. That this activity is contemplative we have already said.[31]

Human good cannot be found in a perfect sense in power or virtue of soul, as these are merely abilities to do something else. Though the body is a good of man, it is not the highest good. The same is true of the soul itself. Happiness is experienced in the soul, but cannot be the soul itself, because people are continually going out of themselves to satisfy the longing of their souls for truth or love.

---

[31] Aristotle, *Nicomachean Ethics*, bk. IX, 7.

The ultimate good of the soul experienced in contemplation is the knowledge of God. But what sort of knowledge of God? There are, in fact, four ways in which we know God. There is the general confused knowledge by which every human being seeks a higher power. No one is naturally an atheist. But this needs to be purified in the knowledge of God through reason, because this confused natural affirmation of God has led some to place the divine in rocks, statues, nature itself, or some other material thing. Socrates purified this idea in Greece by subjecting the gods of the Greek pantheon to rational analysis. He was accused of corrupting the youth by atheism because he held that the Good, or God, must be of a spiritual nature, a metaphysical being. The Scriptures further refined this knowledge of God by faith. This began with revelation of the name YHWH to Moses, which many have interpreted to be the God Aristotle discovered, whose essence is to exist. It is, of course, perfected in Jesus Christ as the prime revealer and revelation of God, the unique mediator. The progressive revelation of God in history ends with the experience of Christ and the death of the last apostle. But this is still not the fullness of our possibility in knowing God, for "faith is the essence of things unseen, the substance of things to be hoped for" (Heb. 11:1). The final completion of our knowledge of God is the vision of the divine essence in Heaven, when man's mind knows the infinity of God without the medium of a concept.

This knowledge completes the longing for truth that began with wonder at the very first experience of cause and effect known by the very first philosopher.

> That men flee from ignorance is clear from this, because those who first philosophized and those who now philosophize begin to philosophize on account of wondering about some cause.... For in the beginning, they wondered about the few doubtful things

which are more at hand so that they might know their causes. Afterwards, from the knowledge of the more manifest things they began to proceed little by little to investigate more hidden things and they began to doubt about the greater and more hidden things (the moon, stars and planets). Some said they were generated by chance, others by mind and others by love.

This wonder was the cause inducing men to philosophize.... The philosophers themselves are moved to philosophize because of wonder at motion. Because wonder proceeds from ignorance, it is clear that men are moved to philosophize that they might flee from ignorance. They love wisdom, not yet possessed in itself. (*In I Meta. III*)

Thirdly, because it is impossible for anyone to obtain perfect happiness except in the vision of the divine essence. This is because the natural desire of the intellect is to understand and know the causes of all things, which is a cause not composed of cause and effect as second causes are. Therefore to take away the possibility of the vision of the divine essence by man is take away happiness itself. Therefore, in order for the created intellect to be happy, it is necessary that the divine essence be seen.[32]

---

[32] "Tertio quia impossibile est quod aliquis perfectam beatitudinem consequatur, nisi in visione divinae essentiae: quia naturale desiderium intellectus est scire et cognoscere causas omnium effectuum cognitorum ab eo; quod non potest impleri nisi scita et cognita prima universali omnium causa, quae non est composita ex effectu et causa, sicut causae secundae. Et ideo auferre possibilitatem visionis divinae essentiae ab hominibus, est auferre ipsam beatitudinem. Necesse est ergo ad beatitudinem intellectus creati, ut divina essentia videatur." Thomas Aquinas, *Comm. In Joann.* I, 11.

The quest for knowledge initiated here cannot end in this life. Philosophers who thought it could were accepting the limitations imposed on human knowledge without grace. "On this point there is abundant evidence of how even the brilliant minds of these men suffered from the narrowness of their viewpoint. From which narrow attitudes we shall be freed if we grant in accord with the foregoing proofs that man can reach true felicity after this life when man's soul is existing immortally, in which state the soul will understand in the way separated substances (angels) understand."[33] Only the Beatific Vision can satisfy the desire of the intellect to understand the causes of the world.

> The conclusion from these considerations is that the ultimate felicity of separate substances does not lie in the knowledge of God, in which they know Him through their substances, for their desire still leads them on toward God's substance. Also, quite apparent in this conclusion is the fact that ultimate felicity is to be sought in nothing other than an operation of the intellect, since no desire carries on to such sublime heights as the desire to understand the truth. Indeed, all our desires for pleasure, or other things of this sort that are craved by men, can be satisfied with other things, but the aforementioned desire does not rest

[33] "In quo satis apparet quantam angustiam patiebantur hinc inde eorum praeclara ingenia. A quibus angustiis liberabimur si ponamus, secundum probationes praemissas, hominem ad veram felicitatem post hanc vitam pervenire posse, anima hominis immortali existente in quo statu anima intelliget per modum quo intelligunt substantiae separatae, sicut in secundo huius operis ostensum est. Erit igitur ultima felicitas hominis in cognitione Dei quam habet humana mens post hanc vitam, per modum quo ipsum cognoscunt substantiae separatae." Aquinas, *Summa Contra Gentiles,* q. 48.

until it reaches God, the highest point of reference for, and the maker of, things. This is why Wisdom appropriately states: "I dwelt in the highest places, and my throne is in a pillar of a cloud" (Sirach 24:7). And Proverbs (9:3) says that Wisdom "by her maids invites to the tower." Let those men be ashamed, then, who seek man's felicity in the most inferior things when it is so highly situated.[34]

Relation of the Final Good to Grace

The concept of the common good is the root of all social order. One cannot distinguish the relation of these goods and their corresponding societies until one has also identified how the ultimate good relates to grace. Since one cannot be fulfilled by any experience here on earth, it would be good to understand how in the Catholic perspective the various experiences of grace in the progressive revelation of God correspond to these goods and thus to the societies that are formed on their basis.

---

[34] "Ex quibus concluditur quod ultima felicitas substantiae separatae non est in illa cognitione Dei qua eum cognoscunt per suas substantias: cum adhuc earum desiderium ducat eas usque ad Dei substantiam. In quo etiam satis apparet quod in nullo alio quaerenda est ultima felicitas quam in operatione intellectus: cum nullum desiderium tam in sublime ferat sicut desiderium intelligendae veritatis. Omnia namque nostra desideria vel delectationis, vel cuiuscumque alterius quod ab homine desideratur, in aliis rebus quiescere possunt: desiderium autem praedictum non quiescit nisi ad summum rerum cardinem et factorem Deum pervenerit. Propter quod convenienter sapientia dicit, Eccli. 24-7: *ego in altissimis habitavi, et thronus meus in columna nubis*. Et Proverb. 9-3 dicitur quod *sapientia per ancillas suas vocat ad arcem*. Erubescant igitur qui felicitatem hominis, tam altissime sitam, in infimis rebus quaerunt." Aquinas, *Summa Contra Gentiles*, q. 50.

Catholic theologians customarily distinguish three states of human nature regarding the relationship of man to grace: Original Justice, Original Sin and Redemption, and Glorified Nature. One cannot understand Christian anthropology, and thus Christian order, unless one understands these three states. St. John Paul II, for instance, demonstrated this truth when he based the division of the first half of his Wednesday audience conferences on sexuality and the community of marriage on these three states. In his parlance, they were: The Original Unity of Man and Woman (Original Justice), Blessed are the Pure of Heart (Original Sin and Redemption), and Virginity and Celibacy for the Sake of the Kingdom (Glorified Nature).[35]

Original Justice, Sin, Redemption, and Glory

The doctrine of Original Justice expresses man as he ought to relate to God in the time before the first sin. Adam and Eve, though individual people, are not treated that way in the first two chapters of the book of Genesis, which St. John Paul II calls "theological prehistory."[36] St. John Paul II also uses the word *myth* to describe this, but this does not mean fabulous content. Rather, it is an attempt to express metaphysical truths that transcend time in sensible terms. In fact, "the whole human race is in Adam 'as one body of one man' " (*CCC* 404). Adam is here not just a representative man but an expression of human nature in relation to God as it ought to be, a truth that underlies the whole of the unfolding of salvation. Adam here is not the first in a series of human beings, but man as he ought to be, looked at from the point of view of God. According to the Council of Trent, man was created in grace. "If anyone does not confess that when Adam

---

[35] John Paul II, *Male and Female He Created Them.*
[36] Ibid., 143.

had transgressed the mandate of God in paradise he did not immediately lose the sanctity and justice in which he had been constituted, anathema sit."[37] This creation in grace was a supernatural condition because Adam was without sin. In addition to this supernatural gift, Adam also enjoyed natural gifts: the intellect, the will, the passions, and the body. That Adam might use these natural gifts to live as he ought through the influence of grace to arrive at the Beatific Vision, God also endowed him with gifts that were beyond (*praeter*) but not above (*super*) his nature. In the intellect, he enjoyed infused knowledge, which is shown in his naming of all the animals in one experience. In the will, he was endowed with loving obedience. God was his intimate friend, and he liked doing the will of God because he understood how this realized his freedom. In the passions, he really enjoyed doing good, and there was no resistance to virtue. He had an easy virtue. This is seen in the fact that the first couple were "naked and were not ashamed" (Gen. 2:25). Adam also did not have any experience of suffering and death, though he had the ability to suffer and die. God preserved him by His external protection from anything that would have caused this. All this depended on an obedience born of love in grace.

> Accordingly man was so constituted that, unless his reason was subservient to God, his body could not be made subject to the beck of his soul, nor his sense powers be brought under the rule of reason. Hence in that state life was in a certain way immortal and impassible; that is, man could neither die nor suffer, so long as he did not sin. Nevertheless he retained the power to sin, since his will was not yet confirmed in good by the

[37] "Primum hominem Adam ... sanctitatem et iustitiam, in qua constitutes fuerat amisse." D. 1511.

attainment of the last end; in the event this happened, man could suffer and die.[38]

This condition will be important for later considerations. For example, would there have been a need for authority or property in this state of perfect man even though there was no sin?

Man had a disordered movement of his will towards himself as though he could persevere in grace, to be God, but "without God, before God and not in accordance with God" (*CCC* 398). In this, he lost grace, and Original Sin entered the human race. Original Sin is not an individual deed done by the first parents, but the condition of losing grace and its aftermath, which results from whatever action was done. "That is why original sin is called 'sin' only in an analogous sense; it is a sin 'contracted' and not 'committed'—a state and not an act" (*CCC* 404).

This introduced into the human race the lack of being created right. By the loss of grace, man loses the proper order of the human person respecting the supernatural order. He turns to a changeable good, as though this could bring him ultimate happiness, and away from the unchangeable good, which is God. This caused man to lose the gifts that depended on this orientation to grace and produced

---

[38] "Ut igitur ratio inferiora sub se firmiter contineret, oportebat quod ipsa firmiter sub Deo contineretur, a quo virtutem praedictam habebat supra conditionem naturae. Fuit ergo homo sic institutus ut nisi ratio eius subduceretur a Deo, neque corpus eius subduci poterat a nutu animae, neque vires sensibiles a rectitudine rationis: unde quaedam immortalis vita et impassibilis erat, quia scilicet nec mori nec pati poterat, si non peccaret. Peccare vero poterat voluntate eius nondum confirmata per adeptionem ultimi finis, et sub hoc eventu poterat mori et pati. Et in hoc differt impassibilitas et immortalitas quam primus homo habuit, ab ea quam in resurrectione sancti habebunt, qui nunquam poterunt nec pati nec mori, voluntate eorum omnino confirmata in Deum." Thomas Aquinas, *Compendium Theologiae*, 186.

inner harmony. In place of infused knowledge, human beings experience ignorance; in place of loving obedience, malice and manipulation; in place of spontaneity in the passions, concupiscence; and in place of no experience of suffering and death, suffering and death. The person becomes like a rebellious city within. Original Justice expressed what man ought to be. His nature becomes fallen. This is what man is now in history that we experience. It was also the nature of man Aristotle and the philosophers experienced. This is man without the organizing principle of his inner self, grace. The supernatural and preternatural gifts are lost. But man is not totally depraved. The natural gifts remain with their natural orientation. The intellect remains oriented to truth; the will to love, the passions to be obedient to reason, and the body ought not to die. Original Sin then is not a personal, a moral, or a juridical condition, but a sin of nature. Thus, all men are implicated in it juridically.

Man after the Original Sin is like an epileptic. He can do some things naturally and well, but not all things. He does not sin in all his acts. Though he does not demerit regarding Hell by the fact of Original Sin, he does not merit arriving at Heaven either. The essence of Original Sin is the lack of grace in the soul, which is expressed subjectively in ignorance, malice, weakness, and death. However, the goods that are characteristic of the natural powers of our souls remain, and these include the "social character," the good of man living in society. Society must exist in either the state of Original Justice or Original Sin. The difference is that society is marred by human egotism after the first sin. It becomes difficult to determine and live the common good. "Many other defects began to appear in man. Inordinate stirrings of passion quickly followed one another in the lower appetites, and at the same time the light of wisdom, which supernaturally illuminated man as long as his will was subordinated to God, grew dim in his intellect. The result of this was that man turned his love to sensible objects. Immersed in these, he wandered far from God and fell into repeated sins."[39]

The redemption wrought by Christ heals this condition of sin. Christ brings back grace, but not the preternatural gifts. Now virtue is not easy, but very difficult. Though human beings are redeemed, they must work out their salvation, addressing their disordered egos. This is painful and is a cross. This also affects both the foundation of society and the way in which human beings morally embrace it. There must be a further society to the one that perfects man in this world that is oriented to redemption. Also, the social character of this society founded on Christ must go beyond exterior conduct and embrace interior conversion. It is the Church, as we shall see later.

Finally, there is human nature, which is characteristic of the final consummation of human powers in the Beatific Vision. This experience of the consummation also has important implications for human nature because this is the perfection of all human powers. The soul is completely brought into perfect act when the cause of all beings is directly experienced without medium in the vision of God. The will rests in joy and love. The passions experience the same joy and love in an emotional way, and the body that is resurrected by miraculous power comes to exist in the manner of the soul, so it cannot die. Though this is the complete fulfillment of man and could be enjoyed if there were only one man who experienced it, there is nonetheless a social union in Heaven because all the angels and saints forever participate and enjoy the same vision together. This is the

[39] "Consecuti sunt in homine per consequens multi alii defectus. Abundantibus enim in appetitu inferiori inordinatis motibus passionum, simul etiam et in ratione deficiente lumine sapientiae, quo divinitus illustrabatur voluntas dum erat Deo subiecta, per consequens affectum suum rebus sensibilibus subdidit, in quibus oberrans a Deo multipliciter peccavit." Aquinas, *Compendium Theologiae*, 194.

final perfection of the Church and is the communion of saints. They offer together the perfect liturgy of praise given to God.

> But if we speak of perfect happiness which will be in our heavenly Fatherland, the fellowship of friends is not essential to happiness; since man has the entire fullness of perfection in God. But the fellowship of friends conduces to the well-being of happiness. Hence, Augustine says that "the spiritual creatures receive no other interior aid to happiness than the eternity, truth and charity of the Creator. But if they can be said to be helped from without, perhaps it is only by this that they see one another and rejoice in God, at their fellowship."[40]

Obviously, the social character does not end in death. The Church exists only perfectly in the communion of saints, which is the most complete realization of the nature of man and yet also of his social nature.

---

[40] "Sed si loquamur de perfecta beatitudine quae erit in patria, non requiritur societas amicorum de necessitate ad beatitudinem, quia homo habet totam plenitudinem suae perfectionis in Deo. Sed ad bene esse beatitudinis facit societas amicorum. Unde Augustinus dicit, VIII super Gen. ad Litt., quod *creatura spiritualis, ad hoc quod beata sit, non nisi intrinsecus adiuvatur aeternitate, veritate, caritate creatoris. Extrinsecus vero, si adiuvari dicenda est, fortasse hoc solo adiuvatur, quod invicem vident, et de sua societate gaudent in Deo.*" Aquinas, *Summa Theologica*, I–II, q. 4, art. 8, ad corp.

TWO

The Social Character and the Origin of Society

The Social Character

Man, by nature, must live in society. In the last chapter, various opinions were discussed as to the origin of this need for society. Some, such as the Marxists and totalitarians, say that society is the substance of man. The social contractualists say that it is merely incidental, or what the Scholastics call an accident.

The definition of the social character depends on how substance and accidents relate to a being in both metaphysics and logic. There are five predicaments in logic: species, genus, difference, property, and accident. The first three of these categories refer to the substance of a thing. The last two reflect the accidents. In philosophy, a substance is a being that exists in its own right; an accident is a being that must exist in another being. A dog or cat are each substances; white, square, and number are accidents.

For Marxists and totalitarians in general, the social character is substantial. Human beings cannot act apart from the collective. All acts are social acts, which are encapsulated in the leader or the people.

One has no individuality. Strictly speaking, there are no private possessions. Man becomes a cog in a giant wheel.

For social contractualists, society is an accident pure and simple. Law, authority, and social relations are purely a matter of choice. The human person remains absolutely free to join society or not. Authority is an imposition on the freedom of the person from outside and is a necessary evil. One can do anything as long as one does not impinge on the freedom of another. Even education is non-directive. There is no real teacher. The teacher is only a facilitator who allows the individual to discover the truth in himself, but never imparts answers or solutions.

Since authority is not necessary, it depends entirely on the will of the people, who can confer it or change it as they see fit. This is also true of the content of laws. There is no objective nature that laws must express, but the subjective will of the completely free person creates the truth, and so morality, day by day.

The solution that the Church has accepted to explain the origin of society is based on a third category: property. A property is not the substance of a thing. It is an accident, but it is not a separable accident. The being cannot exist properly nor be fully understood unless one understands the properties. A property is an accident but not an incidental. In metaphysics, property and accident are both outside a substance and, thus, are both viewed as accidents in the same way. In logic, however, there is a distinction. Property is what is implied in any substance. Pure accident is not so implied.

In man, the substance is man himself, the rational animal composed of body and soul, both of which are necessary to make up the substance. The spiritual soul also makes man a person, which is classically defined as "an individual substance of rational nature." Every man, by nature, has a body, senses, intellect, and will, plus all that is implied in all of these. In this definition, the genus is "animal," the difference is "rational," and the species is man. The social character is not in the genus, species, or difference as such, for it does not make up the actual substance man. One of the properties of a being with an intellect, will, passions, and a body is a sense of humor, or "risibility." Only someone with an intellect can appreciate the difference between what a man is and what he ought to be and find it comic. The passions allow him to enjoy this all the more. Laughter is characteristic of someone who can appreciate the difference in a disinterested way. Yet, human beings are not always laughing. Still, wherever one finds a man, one finds the potential for a sense of humor. The necessity of living in society is the same. Thus, what the essence itself implies is not the essence itself. The statue is not the sculptor, but implies the existence of the sculptor and cannot be found without the sculptor.

Property and accident are outside the substance, but in different ways. Property is found always and only in that species and in every member thereof. An accident is something that can either be or not be a part of a species, and this implies no change in the species. The property does not rise to the status of a substance but flows out from the nature of a given substance. The essence of a thing may imply the existence of the properties but not of the separable accidents. These are, strictly speaking, incidental. Black or white implies nothing to the understanding of the substance man. Being social (i.e., living in society) or anti-social does.

The social character is a characteristic of the spirit that is always implied in the essence of "rational animal." Sexual differentiation is also a property. The manner in which men and women act in a complimentary way is also rooted in the fact that their bodies and chemical structures differ, and the distinctions that emotionally result from this affect the way they approach intellectual study and virtuous development. Though they are equal as to intellect and will, the manner of union of the soul with the body affects study and virtue. This is because knowledge comes through the senses and virtue is lived not only on the level of the will but also on the level of the passions. "For the 'proper' does not belong to the *essence* of a thing, but is *caused* by the *essential* principles of the *species*; wherefore it is a medium between the *essence* and *accident* thus understood. In this sense the powers of the *soul* may be said to be a medium between *substance* and *accident,* as being *natural* properties of the *soul*."[41]

The fact that man is naturally a social animal means that his nature demands the social relationship for perfection. "The human person needs to live in society. Society is not for him an extraneous addition but a requirement of his nature" (CCC 1879).

The fact that he seeks through free will goals like justice, which can only be obtained with other human beings, is the foundation of the social character. Since he has an intellect and will, rapport with others and a social bond are necessary for human perfection and not just a creation of human will. Authority and law in society are necessary for the perfection of this relationship because the will is naturally directed by the intellect. Thus, the will for the common good and the necessity of community flows from the very necessity of wills united in a common goal. The fact of common action to attain this goal is the expression of the social character. Society is thus natural to man, not as a substance, but as a property. Both family and State are natural societies because they perfect something about the human person that cannot be accomplished alone and are necessary for the formation of the virtues in the intellect, will, and passions.

> For it cannot be doubted but that, by the will of God, men are united in civil society; whether its component parts be considered or its form, which implies authority;

---

[41] "Proprium enim non est de essentia rei, sed ex principiis essentialibus speciei causatur, unde medium est inter essentiam et accidens sic dictum. Et hoc modo potentiae animae possunt dici mediae inter substantiam et accidens, quasi proprietates animae naturales." Thomas Aquinas, *Summa Theologica,* I, q. 77, art. 1, ad. 5.

or the object of its existence; or the abundance of the vast services which it renders to man. God it is who has made man for society, and has placed him in the company of others like himself, so that what was wanting to his nature, and beyond is attainment if left to his own resources, he might obtain by association with others. Wherefore, civil society must acknowledge God as its Founder and Parent.[42]

For Hobbes, Rousseau, and the liberal states of the nineteenth century, the social character is a pure accident. For Marx and the totalitarians, it is substantial; it must exist and exhaust every human power regardless of the will of man. For Aristotle, men acting together for the common good naturally do so in social unions. Society perfects man in action according to being, and thus, it belongs to second act. Every community exists for some characteristic good it seeks to inculcate in man by action. This is the good, the perfection, or in the Scholastic sense, the final cause of the society. To understand the nature of a given society and the social order befitting a given society (which includes its authority structure), one must identify its common good. For Aristotle, "he who is unable to live in society, or who has no need because he is sufficient for himself, must be either a beast or a god: he is no part of a state."[43]

Those societies which are oriented to the principal goods of the human race are natural to man. They are two: (1) the domestic family union — the society that perfects procreation and education of human life and leads to the loss of ego in the most direct natural sense; (2) the civil order — the society that perfects man in justice and peace in everyday life.

[42] Leo XIII, encyclical letter *Libertas Praestissimum* (June 20, 1888), no. 21.
[43] Aristotle, *Politics*, 1, 2, 1259a, 28.

And, indeed, nature, or rather God who is the author of nature, wills that man should live in a civil society; and this is clearly shown by the faculty of language, the greatest medium of intercourse, and by numerous innate desires of the mind, and the many necessary things, and things of great importance, which men isolated cannot procure, but which they can procure when joined and associated with others.[44]

The social nature of man shows that there is interdependence between personal betterment and the improvement of society. Insofar as man by his very nature stands completely in the need of life in society, he is and ought to be the beginning, subject and the object of every social organization.[45]

It is traditional in Catholicism to distinguish three basic goods: the monastic good, the domestic good, and the political good. The monastic good is the good of each individual person and is oriented primarily to the development of three cardinal virtues: prudence, temperance, and fortitude. The domestic good is procreation and education of children and unity of the parties involved in this action. Morally, this demands providing for the daily needs of life, which are both temporal and spiritual. The family, on its own level, perfects all four of the cardinal virtues: prudence, justice, temperance, and fortitude. The political good is experienced not only in living, but in living well according to the natural law. The civic community seeks to ensure the domestic good by encouraging the economic order, and to develop the private monastic good by promoting the virtue of justice in the institution of human law.

[44] Leo XIII, encyclical letter *Diuturnum Illud* (June 29, 1881), no. 11.
[45] Vatican Council II, pastoral constitution *Gaudium et Spes* (December 7, 1965), no. 25.

There are many things necessary for human perfection that human beings find difficult to provide for themselves when they live a solitary life. Examples would be shelter, food, protection, and education in prudence and living justice. These are all essential to human perfection, yet human beings usually cannot attain them well alone. Both the State and the family exist to inculcate these goods in their members.

Though the end is very important for determining the ethical good of each society, the various members cannot be sacrificed to it. No social union is so absolute as to be like one physical person with one soul. Nor can the common good of a lower society be sacrificed for a higher good. The domestic order presupposes the moral action of the private individual, and the political order presupposes and nourishes the good of the domestic order. Each order of each society is a true good unto itself.

Plato thought the ideal State was one in which the greatest possible union should occur and that all must be sacrificed to this union. He thus proclaimed the social union of wills to be so absolute that it absorbed the individual will. Because of this, Plato recommended that wives and children be held in common in the ideal State. There was no domestic good apart from the political good. In failing to adequately distinguish between societies and individuals, he compromised the political union as well. It is true that the union of a given society necessarily demands that the human person act by his free choice in a union of wills with other human beings. But this is not so absolute as to destroy the individual or abolish the distinction among the various common goods in which the individual must participate.

Since all these common goods differ, one must respect and guard the other. One cannot supplant another, as Marxists and totalitarians in general insist, without doing violence to both. A person may be an excellent monarch or president but a poor father or mother, and vice versa, a person may be a good man or woman but not a good president or king. There is a real distinction between the domestic good and the political good. This distinction also leads to a real difference in the order, authority, and rule necessary to pursue such goods. What may befit one society may not befit another. This real distinction is rooted in the various levels of man these goods or ends perfect. It is Catholic teaching that both domestic and political communities are natural to man.

The Origin and Definition of Society (Solidarity)

The origin of society is principally in the union of the wills of human persons acting in common. Since the will is the faculty of desire of a reasoning being, this union of action is a reflection of the rational nature of man. Societies cannot be herds, flocks, or faceless masses, since these do not reflect individual human choice. Human beings direct themselves through choice to realizing physical and moral goods. Society is thus not a physical union or absolute unity, but a moral or virtual union. No matter what the purpose, society demands the participation of each member who has chosen to cooperate from knowledge. In a simple example, when ten people row a boat, they must agree on the destination of the trip and how they will row in unison or they will all row at cross-purposes and not go anywhere.

The social contractualists (Hobbes and Rousseau) thought that the origin of society was only found in the free consent of man. Human will created society and law. According to Hobbes, in the primitive state of man, there was no society, no other measure of ethics than what we would view as utilitarianism based on the innate instinct for self-preservation, the war of all against all. To cure this condition, human beings created society and founded the great social institutions. The mind and soul of these societies was the ruler informing and governing all the members of society. Nothing was just by nature. Nothing was just before these societies were founded. The will of the sovereign made something just. This creation was called the "social contract." The contract created justice and authority. What in civil society is called theft, murder, adultery, and lying is not evil by nature, but only by human institution. The civil law determines justice, and there is no prior natural law. Instead, man is by nature a wolf to other men (*homo homini lupus*). Human beings are naturally anti-social. Good and evil are created by human wills.

In this view, the social union is, however, a real union of individual wills. There is no social intellect or will that acts apart from the individuals in the society. Both authority and subject radically retain their personal wills. It is their common moral action for a good pursued in common that is the origin of the social relationship. So their nature as persons is the origin of solidarity.

Rousseau has a variation on the same theme. He taught that man, by nature, is asocial, but not because he is in a state of war. Man was, rather, created in a state of friendship. Man, in the beginning, led a life of contentment, with no desires, envies, or struggles. In this state of happiness, he developed art, agriculture, class, property, and riches little by little. It is because of these things that discord entered the human race. To do away with this evil condition, human beings were forced to freely found the social contract. This pact was fixed in the people who made it and was inalienable and indivisible. Law receives its sanction from the universal will of the people. The people thus confer all the power and sanction on the sovereign. They, therefore, can remove the power for the slightest cause and even execute the ruler. Every citizen clings to the social contract like a plank in a shipwreck. The origin of society is wholly in the collective will of the people.

The general position of the popes is very different from social contract theory. The final cause of society, which is the goal for which a society is founded, is the common good. This common good in the domestic and political orders is natural to man. The origin of society is thus founded in the fact that men are neither natural enemies nor naturally completely autonomous. Rather, the social relation is founded on the necessity of human wills acting in concert to obtain a good that they could not easily attain by themselves. To be a person entails participation in society. For Christianity, this is obviously seen primarily in God, Who is not an autonomous solitary. God is a communion of Persons Who are completely united in a communion of knowledge and love for all eternity. This is the archetype of all society. The Persons are radically distinct and yet radically united with each other. The origin of society is thus primarily in the natural order based on the objective nature of a person possessing an intellect and will. Since the Godhead is made up of the three primary Persons and they are the authors and founders of the natural order, the primary source of all society is God through the natural order.

> But God has likewise destined man for civil society according to the dictates of his very nature. In the plan of the Creator, society is a natural means which man can and must use to reach his destined end. Society is for man and not vice versa. This must not be understood in the sense of liberalistic individualism, which subordinates society to the selfish use of the individual; but only in the sense that by means of an organic union with society and by mutual collaboration the attainment of earthly happiness is placed within the reach of all.[46]

Society has been defined as "the unity of order of human persons united in origin and purpose and acting in common."[47] In this defini-

---

[46] Pius XI, encyclical letter *Divini Redemptoris* (March 19, 1937), no. 29.

[47] "Adunatio hominum ad unum aliquid communiter agendum." Thomas Aquinas, *Contra Impugnantes Cultum Dei*, co 5.

tion, *Adunatio* represents the fact that the social union is not merely in the mind but is a real moral union of wills acting together. *Hominum* expresses the fact that society is a moral and virtual union of human beings acting for a common goal that is rooted in the spiritual nature of man. *Agendum* identifies this action as one oriented to ethical perfection of the soul and thus perfecting the interior powers of the soul as opposed to an artifact. Society is an application of ethics and not of art in the ancient sense. *Ad unum aliquid* defines the nature of a given society as based on the particular ethical purpose that the common good sought in that society perfects. *Communiter* shows that though the origin of society is human nature, its perfection in action cannot be taken for granted. Each member must freely participate in seeking the common good on which the society is based in solidarity if such a social order is to flourish.

Pius XII expressed it this way: "Order, the basis of social life among men — among intelligent and responsible beings, that is, who pursue an end appropriate to their nature — is not a mere extrinsic connection between parts numerically distinct; it tends towards an ever more perfect achievement of internal unity, a unity however, which does not exclude differences in reality and sanctioned by the will of the Creator and by supernatural laws."[48]

Society is a real union of relationships of willed action among intelligent individuals. It is also a unity of order based on some specific object, not a mere plurality or union found only in the mind. It is not the kind of absolute unity found in one person, so there is no such thing as a collective will or intellect. In society, the part can have an action different from the whole. But when it is a question of the specific good sought in the society, then certain actions must be done or avoided. In the example of a group of people rowing a boat, each may study a

---

[48] Pius XII, Christmas Broadcast (1942).

different subject, love a different person or love no person, have different physical or emotional qualities, like different foods, and profess different religions. But unless they all row together toward a chosen destination, they will not win the race or arrive at any destination. They will row endlessly at cross-purposes and get nowhere. Society must be a union of action with a certain order.

The Common Good

A person realizes himself in acting in common with others and still maintaining his identity and uniqueness; otherwise there is absolute uniformity, which is not order but disorder, since it fails to take account of different contributions and services vital to the realization of the goal. In a true social union, the human person does not give up his individuality but realizes it. Participation in society refers to the fact that human beings act together to better realize their freedom for a certain good. "The trait of participation thus indicates that man, when he acts together with other men, retains in this acting the personalistic value of his own action and at the same time shares in the realization and the results of communal action. Reversing this sequence we may say that owing to this share man, when he acts together with others, retains everything that results from the communal acting and at the same time realizes — in this very manner — the personalistic value of his action."[49]

Social participation means the members of a society are not just a herd of mindless beings acting to the stimulus and response of the controlling authority. Social action has to be a result of an interior choice for those who are able to make freely willed choices. This would, of course, involve some level of understanding of the nature of the

[49] Karol Wojtyła, *The Acting Person*, trans. Andrzej Potocki (London: D. Reidel Publishing Company, 1979), 325.

good pursued in the society and interior choice of it. This is a further application of the principle that society is a "property" of man. "Participation thus represents a *property* of the person himself, that inner and homogeneous property which determines that the person existing and acting together with others still exists and acts as a person.... Under certain conditions "acting" (as a synonym of "action") may change into something that only "happens" to a particular man under the influence of other men. An extreme example of this is so-called "mass psychology," when a large group of men may begin to act in an uncontrolled way and so affect the behavior of individuals."[50]

Thus, the social relationship does not destroy individuality but exists to serve individuality on a deeper level of the soul. The perfection and order of the community differs from a natural order in the sense that man must interest himself in realizing the goal of social union by participation. The order of the community is the work of man and always has a moral character. Everything in the community presupposes a common nature (human nature, to be a person, to have reason) that is spiritual and perfects the soul. This, in turn, is the source of the moral participation of the members. The person is the origin of the social relationship in those acts that are characteristic of one who has a reasoning soul. Using practical reason, persons in society try to implement a good together. The common good willed creates the kind of community, and the good of the community must always be in accord with human nature. So, it always has some relationship to morals. A community must not direct itself to an end that is evil. This would destroy the members of the community morally. The community may permit immoral actions by choosing not to punish them, if this would compromise a greater good or lead to a greater evil. But the community cannot give evil rights.

[50] Ibid., 326.

In an authentic human community, each person must maintain the freedom that is based on his nature and place and realize this on a deeper level in the common action. A community does not act as such, but the members act in the name of the community. The solidarity that is caused by the common good also presupposes a given order. This order, like society, also "exists for man and not vice versa."[51] "The attitude of solidarity is, so to speak, the natural consequence of the fact that human beings live and work together; it is the attitude of a community, in which the common good properly conditions and initiates participation and participation in turn properly serves the common good, fosters it, and furthers its realization. Solidarity signifies a constant readiness to accept and to realize one's share in the community — what is one's share because of one's membership in a particular community."[52]

The common good must, therefore, include both the end and order of the community. The end would be first in intention and last in execution and would be primarily identified in the intellect by understanding how a specific good sought related to human nature. This is the order of intention in the Scholastic sense. The order used to attain this good would be in the execution of the good and so implements the means. These would be first here, and the end would be the last thing realized. This would take place in the will.

The order exists for the sake of the end, and every end must have an order that befits it because a given order makes realizing the end more expedient. As both entail the common good, both have certain necessary human characteristics. Both end and order must (1) be morally good or at least neutral, (2) be a real common good that transcends the mere selfish interest or agenda of one group in society, and (3) respect a proper relationship with other values that are more properly willed in

---

[51] Pius XI, *Divini Redemptoris*, no. 29.
[52] Karol Wojtyła, *The Acting Person*, 341.

other societies and are also necessary to human perfection. The common good cannot then just be the sum of the private material goods of the majority of the individuals in society. "Thus the priority of the common good, its superiority over the partial or individual goods does not result solely from the quantitative aspect of the society; it does not follow from the fact that the common good concerns a great number of the majority while the individual good concerns only individual or a minority. It is not the numbers or even the generality in the quantitative sense but the intrinsicalness that determines the proper nature of the common good."[53]

In the same way that the end and order of the community condition and supplement each other, the common good and individual good also do so. There can be no community when there is no common good that can be agreed upon and so willed by the members. The community must have the same goal as the individual member. However, the good of the individual must be subordinated to the common good because it is this deeper good that allows the individual to attain some perfection in acting that would not be possible otherwise.

Since the common good includes both the intellect and will, though society is generally concerned with enacting justice and charity (virtues found in the will), prudence is absolutely necessary. Ruling and governing human beings is an application of prudence and must involve intelligence and truth. The unity of the goal first willed, and then executed by an appropriate means in action, does not destroy the nature of the individual but rather redounds to the realization of some power of the human soul in being. Another way to put this is that living a true community order pursuant of a correct human end fulfills the individual. This is true, though it may limit the freedom of the possible choices the individual makes.

Social unity, then, is not a physical or material union but a virtual and habitual union, a moral and intentional unity that seeks to

[53] Ibid., 340.

implement a further experience of existing by the perfection of the human powers of the soul of the individuals. This good unites the members of a given society in a variety of ways. It perfects each of them in their individual personalities since they will it freely. Though the natural common good truly perfects the human soul, it can never exhaust the transcendental nature of a spiritual being such as man. The only good that can do this is a supernatural one.

Both the end and the order must be maintained for the common good to exist. If one tries to attain the end without the order, then it causes chaos. If one seeks only to affirm the order without a human end, it ends in slavery. Order can never be a final purpose in itself. It is always a means. In totalitarian communities, order is an end in itself. This is also true of exaggerated bureaucracies that exist to perpetuate themselves and whose very complication frustrates the good that such an order was founded to attain. In social contract communities, the end and the order are simply the creation of the sum of the material private goods of the individuals in society.

This book has been treating of those communities that are necessary for human life. There is another kind of community that is based on friendship, or on cooperation, that is not formal and seeks a common good that is truly accidental to human perfection. Examples of this might be stamp collecting clubs or card clubs. These are purely the creation of the human will and are oriented to goods that have no necessary relation to realizing something deeper in the human person. The common good and order in this case would be something that a person can take or leave and his nature would still be whole and complete.

Common Good versus "Mass" Men

In the nineteenth and twentieth centuries, various theories of the origin of society gave rise to a kind of treatment of the human person that was based on materialism and relativism. This was caused by a

denial of a realistic, objective metaphysics espoused by Enlightenment philosophers such as Kant, Rousseau, and Hume. Coupled
with this position about the inability of physics to discover any but
mathematical or material motion is the final revolution in thought
in the twentieth century caused by the discovery of relativity by
Einstein. This completely discredited the mathematical physics of
Newton as entailing fixed and inalterable perfect laws in the universe. In the law of unintended consequences, Einstein watched in
horror as his theory that introduced relativity in physics eventually
undercut all certain truths in ethics and religion. Paul Johnson has
characterized this final nail in the coffin of a science that could lead
to truths about God and the preamble to realistic metaphysics and
ultimately to faith:

> At the beginning of the 1920's the belief began to circu-
> late, for the first time at a popular level, that there were
> no longer any absolutes: of time and space, of good and
> evil, of knowledge, but above all of value. Mistakenly
> but perhaps inevitably relativity became confused with
> relativism. No one was more distressed than Einstein by
> this public misapprehension.... He wrote a colleague
> Max Born on 9 September 1920: "Like the man in the
> fairy-tale who turned everything he touched into gold,
> so with me everything turns into a fuss in the news-
> papers." ... He lived to see moral relativism, to him a
> disease, become a social pandemic, just as he lived to
> see his fatal equation bring into existence nuclear war-
> fare. There were times, he said at the end of his life, he
> wished he had been a simple watchmaker.[54]

[54] Paul Johnson, *Modern Times* (New York: Harper Perennial, 1983), 4.

Nor was this all. The beginning of the twentieth century also saw the full implications of the denial of personal responsibility, which was heralded by Sigmund Freud in his discovery of neuroses. Freud's theory of psychoanalysis sounded the death knell for the responsibility of the personal conscience in moral actions, since it basically attributed moral behavior to a series of unconscious forces that ranged from repressed sexuality to the death wish. Again, Paul Johnson summarizes this well: "Equally, in Freudian analysis, the personal conscience, which stood at the very heart of the Judeo-Christian ethic, and was the principal engine of individualistic achievement, was dismissed as a mere safety-device, collectively created, to protect civilized order from the fearful aggressiveness of human beings."[55]

The twentieth century was thus characterized by relativism in truth, both in nature and in morals, which has led to many political and social theories that deny the objective inviolability of the human person and seek a collectivism or totalitarianism that reduces individuals to a faceless mass. Mass psychology and manipulation have replaced presentation of the truth to individuals and the recognition that individuals choose to act in common. It is true that the common good has a sanction over and above merely the individual good. But it does not demand that all individuals be subsumed into it so they have no radical individuality. Society must respect all the individual goods as vital because society and the social good seek to perfect the individuals in it according to what is higher in their nature.

> Society is willed by the Creator as a means to the full development of the faculties of the individual, and a man has to make use of society now giving and again taking for his own good and for the good of others. Even more, those higher and more universal values which

[55] Ibid., 10.

cannot be realized by individuals but only by society are
intended by the Creator ultimately for the sake of the
ultimate end of man, for his natural and supernatural
development and perfection. Whoever transgresses
this order shakes the pillars of society and imperils its
tranquility, security, and even its existence.[56]

Once people surrender the metaphysical truth that each human person
is a unique individual because of the spiritual soul, the value of the
person is lost and people become a herd of material individuals without
a spiritual inner dimension. "Mass" man enters the picture. The word
mass can have two meanings. It can mean merely a large majority of
people, as in the case of employers, teachers, workers, and the faithful.
This makes no judgment on the individual. It can also be taken to mean
that people have a common experience, or history, or class consciousness. Again, since this implies nothing about the inner nature of man
and can be used to encourage people to the higher perfections of their
nature, this sense is fine and good. This second meaning, however,
may be used to deny individuality by appealing only to a kind of mass
psychology. Mob psychology is based on this, where people are not
encouraged to critically think but merely to indulge in a general mood
created and manipulated by clever group dynamics.

This second sense is the most destructive of true social union and,
unfortunately, has come to characterize the thinking of the modern
age. People are just swept along by the climate of public opinion often
created by a manipulative media or education system with no interest in the objective truth. Indeed, objective truth is denied. Given
the propensity of the media and education to deemphasize the fact
of objective truth with such powerful tools as the internet and mass

---

[56] Pius XI, encyclical letter *Mit Brennender Sorge* (March 14, 1937), no. 34.

communications, it is no wonder that there is an almost global tendency to mass psychology that can be influenced to think in a certain way just because it is the commonly perceived wisdom.

When Catholics want to make doctrine and morals a matter of "common" ground produced in mass media manipulated by group dynamics with no proper discussion of truth, this demonstrates the universality of the phenomenon. The practice of contraception, which leads to eugenics, abortion, and euthanasia, has further deadened people to the moral nature of their individual choices and their freedom. Dr. Conrad Baars was sent to the concentration camp of Buchenwald for a number of years. He reflects on how the moral desertion of the collective "mass" man produced by the implementation of contraception in France contributed to the "survival of the fittest" mentality there.

> Once on the battlefields of World War I, now in the concentration camps of World War II, France paid its price for taking the lead in one of the most successful campaigns in modern history some one hundred and twenty years earlier: the campaign of birth control. Successful their campaign had been, because birth control appeals so much to the selfish element in every human being. It eliminates the responsibilities and duties of love, it decries the consequence of romance, and it educates young people in their selfish interest and in the indulgence of their selfish pleasures. France, by destroying the morality of its youth, had led the way to the destruction of its own existence; it had removed in its children the backbone of perseverance against evil. They had nobody to blame but themselves, not even their executioners, the Communists, who were only

supporting Malthus' theory that the mad, rabbit-like multiplication of the members of the human race would cause disastrous exhaustion of the world's food supply.[57]

The denial of metaphysical truth reduces man to a collective mass in which the only appeal is to a kind of order and unity in society that refuses to respect differences. The collective abrogates to itself the complete re-appropriation of the nature of law and justice so that there is no appeal outside the collective will, whether this is exercised by a king, an aristocracy, a democracy, or a dictator. Human beings are reduced to state planning, and truth is determined by the majority. In religion, this even becomes true of doctrinal truth.

Though it is true that the common good has a useful aspect to it because the order respects means to an end, the means cannot predominate over the end. When the State, for example, wants to be father, teacher, priest, employer, and physician at the expense of all other social entities, arbitrary usurpations of power take place. This is also true in exaggerated bureaucracies where the perpetuation of the bureau becomes more important than the people it is meant to serve. This amounts to turning means into ends and has been endlessly pursued throughout the twentieth century and the beginning of the twenty-first by things like fascism, Nazism, five-year plans, and socialized medicine. The common good of the community must lead it not to replace its parts but to encourage them to act on their own.

The common good, then, must always be according to human nature. The good of the whole cannot be pursued at the expense of the part but must respect and promote that good. This is especially true of the higher community seeking to supplant the lower community.

[57] Conrad Baars, *Doctor of the Heart* (New York: Alba House, 1996), 110.

Instead of substitution, the higher good must encourage the lower, except in the case of extreme emergency, and only then on a temporary basis. Only this can guarantee freedom and individuality to the members. "The higher the values, the greater the liberty required."[58] The Church must have more freedom than economic communities, and the family than the artistic community. One should not seek to deny the existence and proper action of the lower community except in case of extreme emergency, such as a famine. The State, for example, must respect the circumstances of the particular time and place. If in an epidemic, vaccination and quarantine are required, these should not be extended needlessly beyond the time of the epidemic.

The community, then, does not exist to deny the rights of the individual but to promote them. The common good exists not to make people mindless ciphers of the collective but to encourage people to morally responsible behavior in which they freely embrace the common values. "The political community exists for the common good: this is its full justification and meaning and the source of its specific and basic right to exist. The common good embraces the sum total of all those conditions of social life which enable individuals, families, and organizations to achieve complete and efficacious fulfillment."[59]

---

[58] Eberhard Welty, *Man in Society*, vol. 1, *A Handbook of Christian Social Ethics* (Freiberg, West Germany: Herder and Herder, 1960), 113.

[59] Vatican Council II, *Gaudium et Spes*, no. 74.

THREE

The Origin and Nature of Authority

All Authority Is from God

Many people today are very confused about the origin of authority and thus the obligation to form their conscience according to the judgments of authority. This also has its source in the denial of metaphysical truths and thus the denial of God as the author of the being and truth of the universe. The traditional way to describe God's relationship with the truth in the world is to state that the ideas in the mind of God are the origin of truth in all the things that He has made. Those things themselves are the origin of the truth about them reflected in the human mind. The human mind measures and creates no truth about natural things. Man's mind merely discovers the truth in things. This includes the truth of human nature.

Since the Enlightenment, due to a denial of a realistic objective metaphysics, the opposite has been the case. When scientists discovered that, through reason, many things once thought mysterious could be controlled and developed for human purposes of progress, they were justly impressed with human reason. But they then drew the exaggerated conclusion that the progress of human reason could solve all human problems and plumb the depths of the mysteries of the universe to control and dominate it. Knowledge became power and theoretical truth was reduced to the practical order of control and domination. Man's truth became the source of the truth of things. The things as created by man became the standard by which to measure the truth of all things, even the truth of God. God must justify Himself to man for man to believe in Him. The title of C. S. Lewis's book *God in the Dock* reflects this attitude. The "dock" is where the accused stands in an English courtroom. God becomes the accused and must demonstrate to man why man should acknowledge His existence according to the standards of human progress created by reason.

The effect of this on authority, conscience, and obedience is radical. In traditional philosophy and religion, God is the source of all authority. He does not govern His creation directly but through secondary causes. He does not directly heat water but uses fire. He uses the energy from the sun as the source of energy on earth. In a similar way, God governs human beings but through secondary causes, which are the human authorities in human communities.

There is, therefore, an analogy between the natural universe and the moral universe. They are both governed by God through secondary causes. In the natural universe, the intermediary cause is determined according to power in a kind of hierarchy. The most powerful source of energy imparts energy to all the beings that participate in this, and sources of energy participate more insofar as they contain the power of energy in themselves. In the moral universe, it is not the most powerful as to the form of a being that determines the source of God's governance. Rather, the source of governance in the moral universe is the most powerful according to truth and goodness. Authority is determined by the one who represents the more universal truth and the more universal common good. The common good of the Church is of a significantly different character than the common good of the State. It is not inimical to the good of the State, but it is of a higher order, as it is only finally experienced in Heaven in the vision of God in the communion of saints. The common good of the State is of a higher order than that of the family, though its purpose is not to supplant the family. The common good of the economic community or business is an adjunct good to the good of the family. Through the family wage and the goods and services provided by the business community, the family is sustained. This is necessary for the good development of the State. Other unnecessary communities are determined by how central their good is to the human good as a whole.

Since every society is ordered to a particular realization of the common good that is primarily attained by the desire of the will, every society depends on intelligence and reason to present the prospective goods to the will. The will is like the feet pursuing the good, but the intellect is like the eyes by which the person knows where he is going while he is walking. The intellect presents the good to the will, and if the will is open to it, the person pursues the good. Intelligence is, therefore, the most basic origin of authority, although, of course, it is implemented by the will, the central power of morals. Obedience is also more involved with the intellect than the will. The good is carried out by the will but at the direction of the truth presented. The word *obedience* comes from *obaudire*, which means "on account of hearing." This suggests that obedience is more a matter of the intellect than the will. The interpretation that views authority as a competition of wills in which the intelligence is not really involved is neither Catholic nor good philosophy.

On the question of the origin of authority, there are two incorrect schools of thought. The first places the origin of authority in the human will alone. The strongest will creates justice and good. In an age that rejects an objective metaphysics, the aspect of the all-powerful will bearing no restraint but what the person places on himself is a natural idea. The other is that since authority is primarily a matter of the will and since the man we experience in everyday life has a fallen nature, there would have been no authority needed before the existence of sin. Authority is a result of sin.

Both of these ideas are mistaken precisely because authority is primarily a matter of the intellect. Truth directs the good and comes before it. This is why no authority, no matter how powerful its will, can make something wrong right or can be said to govern properly if the subjects are treated as animals, as having no will of their own. No authority can claim that there need be no explanation given of possible commands. The origin of authority would thus be the need for any group of people, no matter how innocent, to need directing in pursuing a common good. The example is clear again in rowing the boat. If there are ten people rowing the boat and they are told they all may exercise their freedom as to how, when, and in what direction they shall row, they won't achieve any objective. Someone must be designated to at least help them decide on a common destination and row together towards that place.

The point becomes clear in an examination of the issue of whether there would have been authority needed in the state of Original Justice, when there was no sin. What would be its nature and how would it be structured? The Church has generally accepted the understanding that since man is naturally a social animal and since the union of wills in pursuit of the common good must be directed by the intellect, authority would be necessary in any society. The necessity of authority does not, therefore, come from Original Sin because of the egotistical tendencies of men. "But as no society can hold together unless someone be over all, directing all to strive earnestly for the common good, every body politic must have a ruling authority, and this authority, no less than society itself, has its source in nature, and has, consequently, God for its Author."[60]

There was some disagreement over the nature and origin of authority in the state of innocence. St. Augustine has often been cited as holding the opinion in book XIX chapter 19 of The *City of God* that because slavery is a creation of sin, so is the dominion of authority. He is often contrasted with St. Thomas, who, because of the influence of Aristotle, held in his most mature works that there would have been authority in Eden.[61]

To understand the full weight of the Catholic tradition on this subject, it is important to examine the nuances St. Thomas makes in his opinions on this subject. First, St. Augustine was right that the dominion that one man exercises over another expressed in the institution of slavery is not in the original creation of Adam and Eve, who were given dominion over the world and the plants and animals, but that specific dominion over man was the result of human artifice in light of the Original Sin. The cause was economic development in the ancient world. St. Thomas designates this as an example of the *Ius Gentium*, which is an extension of the natural law in which human beings seek to put general necessities of life into practice by their reason. Property is a creation of this also as a result of the Original Sin. The fact of slavery as practiced for most of the history of the world does

---

[60] Leo XIII, encyclical letter *Immortale Dei* (November 1, 1885), no. 3. Pope Leo also teaches in another place: "But now, a society can neither exist nor be conceived in which there is no one to govern the wills of individuals, in such a way as to make, as it were, one will out of many, and to impel them rightly and orderly to the common good; therefore, God has willed that in a civil society there should be some to rule the many." Encyclical letter *Diuturnum Illud* (June 29, 1881), no. 11.

[61] For example, Paul J. Weithman, "Augustine and Aquinas on Original Sin and the Function of Political Authority," *Journal of the History of Philosophy*, Internet Project Muse, 353–75.

not mean it is a true good in accord with reason, but merely that human beings for many centuries thought it was the only way to ensure economic prosperity. It is in fact evil.

What sort of dominion was exercised in Eden? St. Thomas takes up this question in general in an early work, The *Commentary on the Sentences of Peter Lombard*, and then develops his more mature idea of it in his *Summa Theologica*. His basic ideas and distinctions on this subject do not change from his original to his more mature thought.

St. Thomas first makes a distinction between two ways in which one exercises authority over another: one is to govern others in general (*ad regimen ordinatus*); the other is to dominate over others (*ad dominandum*).[62] The difference is found in a teaching of Aristotle concerning the difference between a ruler and a tyrant. A ruler seeks the common good; a tyrant seeks his own private good. "Therefore he intends the good of the ones subject to authority; in the second the personal good of the one exercising authority."[63] The second way of ruling did not exist in the state of innocence except regarding animals that have no reasoning nature.

St. Thomas lists four ways in which the act of ruling is applied in a society. The first is directing the members of the society in what they should do. The second is to supply for difficulties (as in national defense). The third is to correct morals by punishment, and the fourth is to use coercion to lead people to virtuous acts.[64] The last two actions of authority

---

[62] Thomas Aquinas, *Scriptum Super Libros Sententiarum*, II, d. 44, q. 1, art. 3, co.

[63] "Quia in primo intenditur bonum subditorum, in secundo proprium bonum praesidentis." Ibid.

[64] "Sed prima praelatio, quae ordinatur ad utilitatem subditorum, fuisset ibi quantum ad aliquem usum, non quantum ad omnes. Est enim praelatio, ad dirigendum subditos in his quae agenda sunt, et ad supplendum defectus, ut quod populi a regibus defendantur; et iterum ad corrigendum mores, dum mali puniuntur, et coacte ad actus virtutis inducuntur." Ibid.

would not have been necessary in the state of innocence because there was no sin and no moral weakness to correct. The direction of authority, however, in the first two instances, directing others as to knowledge and action would have been necessary. This is because there was no absolute equality even in the state of innocence, as some people were more intelligent and more virtuous than others. Before the first sin, the most virtuous and suitable person would have been chosen to exercise authority. Such is not the case after the first sin. People unsuited to the task often exercise authority for various reasons. In the family, this is determined by an order of wise governor to free citizen regarding husband and wife. This has been perverted into master for slave because of the desire to dominate that characterizes Original Sin. In the State, the most prudent and virtuous person would have been chosen to exercise authority. After the first sin, people often become tyrants who exercise authority.

One should notice also that the coercive power needed by any authority is only a result of Original Sin, and this reflects an interior disorder, just as Original Justice reflects an interior order. Man was created in grace. This in no sense altered his nature. The social nature of man described by no less a person than Aristotle would not have been altered by this creation but enhanced by it. The interior order of the soul wrought by not only grace but the union of knowledge, love, passions, and no death through the special gifts given to man by God would have been the basis for real and deep social relations in all the social experiences of such persons. When this union was lost by disobedience through the loss of grace, these special gifts were lost, and the loss of these affected all social relationships. What before would have been an expression of unity in the Holy Trinity and characterized by gift and reception after the manner of the persons of the Trinity now degenerates into mutual extortion and a desire for power. This is seen especially in marriage but also would have affected politics and friendship. Authority now enters not just to direct man to good deeds but also to have sanctions that keep people from making others objects of use.

In the state of innocence, then, there would have been human authority based on the natural preeminence in virtue of one man over another. Indeed, if a man is especially prudent, it is most fitting for him to use his gifts for the service of others. Though this involves implementing justice, it is actually found in the practical intellect, which is perfected by prudence. With Aristotle, St. Thomas gives one of the principle expressions of prudence as "regnative prudence," which has to do with the art of ruling another. One who so enjoys an intense integration of truth and love in practice has an obligation to use this for the service of others. When many have to act as one, the direction of an authority is needed.

> But a man is the master of a free subject, by directing him either towards his proper welfare, or to the common *good*. Such a kind of mastership would have *existed* in the state of innocence between *man* and *man*, for two reasons.
>
> First, because *man* is *naturally* a social being, and so in the state of innocence he would have led a social life. Now a social life cannot *exist* among a number of people unless under the presidency of one to look after the common *good*; for many, as such, seek many things, whereas one attends only to one. Wherefore the *Philosopher* says, in the beginning of the *Politics*, that wherever many things are directed to one, we shall always find one at the head directing them.
>
> Secondly, if one *man* surpassed another in *knowledge* and *virtue*, this would not have been fitting unless these *gifts* conduced to the benefit of others, according to *1*

Peter 4:10, "As every *man* hath received *grace,* ministering the same one to another." Wherefore *Augustine* says (*De Civ. Dei* xix, 14): "Just men command not by the love of domineering, but by the service of counsel": and (*De Civ. Dei* xix, 15): "The *natural* order of things requires this; and thus did *God* make *man.*"[65]

Human societies are of many kinds, but all need direction. That direction is caused by being able to implement ideas about man in general to his specific moral practice and so to develop each person's character in the given circumstances of everyday life. The need for direction by authority does not free the directee from participating in this direction from his own particular choice. It is, rather, an application of both conscience and prudence. Conscience and prudence have some things in common and some differences. They are both about applying right reason in action. Conscience ends in a judgment in the intellect, and a person may choose to act against his conscience in the will. Prudence, however, includes the application of truth to practice in the will. The order of a society is oriented to the development of conscience in action of each member of that society, but then also to actually apply

[65] "Primo quidem, quia homo naturaliter est animal sociale, unde homines in statu innocentiae socialiter vixissent. Socialis autem vita multorum esse non posset, nisi aliquis praesideret, qui ad bonum commune intenderet, multi enim per se intendunt ad multa, unus vero ad unum. Et ideo philosophus dicit, in principio Politic., quod quandocumque multa ordinantur ad unum, semper invenitur unum ut principale et dirigens. Secundo quia, si unus homo habuisset super alium supereminentiam scientiae et iustitiae, inconveniens fuisset nisi hoc exequeretur in utilitatem aliorum; secundum quod dicitur I Petr. IV, *unusquisque gratiam quam accepit, in alterutrum illam administrantes.* Unde Augustinus dicit, XIX de Civ. Dei, quod *iusti non dominandi cupiditate imperant, sed officio consulendi, hoc naturalis ordo praescribit, ita Deus hominem condidit.*" Thomas Aquinas, *Summa Theologica,* I, q. 96, co.

this to his will in his actions. The authority must be able to do both. As the flautist is to the flute maker, so is the authority to the subject. The one directs and the other implements using both the intellect and will to direct and to apply.

In a state, for instance, both the rulers and the subjects are citizens. Though the ruler gives direction, he is not the state. The captain, the pilot, and the cook are sailors, and so both the ruler and the subject serve the order of the society, each doing his part. If either the captain or the pilot or the cook fail in their duties, the ship will not reach port. *Citizen* is a common term that expresses many different functions in realizing the common good. Each must serve in his place, and there is a prudence proper to each. The same would be true in the family.

The common work is the common action needed for the health and safety of the community as it pursues its goal. Each common virtue of the community depends on the kind of government that the citizens elect. The virtue of prudence would be developed different in a democracy, oligarchy, or monarchy. Also, there is proper prudence that must be developed for each person as an individual in actions apart from the community. Aristotle distinguishes political prudence in the State from domestic prudence in the family and monastic prudence, which is the prudence of the individual. A person may, for instance, have the prudence of a good citizen but not be a good man. This is because the monastic good is not the same as the common good. Even in the best State, it is necessary that each have the virtue of a good citizen but not necessarily of a good man. The citizens must know how to obey the laws even if their hearts are not in it.

Every order creates similarity from dissimilar things, such as the order in an animal or a man. The prudence of the ruler is not the same as the prudence of the subject. For example, in a choir, the expertise of the choirmaster is not the same as the singer. Nor is the expertise of the conductor in the orchestra the same as the first violinist. The conductor must lead the orchestra by keeping them together and realizing the score. Each member of the orchestra must play his instrument well by following the lead of the conductor. The members of the orchestra do not have to have the ability to lead the orchestra. On the other hand, if they fail to follow the lead of the conductor, even if they play their instrument well, they will not produce music but noise.

Christian social order has always recognized politics is the art of prudence. The prudence of a ruler and of a good man go together in office for a man to be able to direct others well. Still, the subject is not just a puppet who is absolved from personal responsibility in carrying out the commands of authority. It is no defense in committing evil for the evildoer to claim he was just following orders. If the individual citizen perceives that an order given by authority is evil, he has a moral obligation not to obey such a law, as it can in no way represent the common good.

The art of prudence is especially realized for those in charge of the community by making good laws and the practical ability to implement them. Rulers who make laws are like architects making plans for buildings. They give direction and order to the craftsmen according to their preconceived plan.

However, if the craftsmen are poor, the building will fall down no matter how skilled the architect. The subjects, therefore, also have to exercise the virtue of prudence when they consent to put the laws into practice. In this, they realize the plan of the architect. Modern ideas of prudence would suggest that the most prudent person is the one who avoids as much involvement in the community as possible. The modern notion of the prudent person is one who minds his own business and only becomes interested when he is forced to do so. Often, that involvement is a mindless application of the rules with no thought to the purpose. Though leaders are more responsible for the good of the community than the subject, since prudence has to do with the singular ultimate, each member is responsible for carrying out his part as freely as possible.

Though the good of society must be in accord with the natural law and no authority can command something contrary to the natural law, there are times when a given society must permit evils to exist in order to efficaciously further the common good, when the attempt to suppress all evil would lead to a greater harm to a higher good or promote a greater evil. In this, human law and authority take their cue from God. "God, despite his omnipotence and supreme goodness, allows evils he could prevent to exist in the world, if removing them would cause greater goods to be lost or greater evils to ensue. So human rulers may also tolerate some evils for the same reasons; 'forbid prostitution,' says Augustine, 'and lust will turn everything upside down.' The religious rites of unbelievers, though sinful, can be tolerated if doing so brings good and avoids evil."[66] Authority may never command immorality, but it may choose not to punish immorality.

Prudence in government is more than just using general conclusions applied without thought and discretion to individual circumstances. In fact, such prudence is rarely found in young people regarding others, because they lack experience and their decisions are often affected by their passions. In social discourse, this means understanding how, in practice, one unifies many disparate temperaments and experiences to constitute a whole, to form one principle or subject of action. The officers in the army, from the commissioned to non-commissioned,

---

[66] "Sic igitur et in regimine humano illi qui praesunt recte aliqua mala tolerant, ne aliqua bona impediantur, vel etiam ne aliqua mala peiora incurrantur, sicut Augustinus dicit, in II de ordine, *aufer meretrices de rebus humanis, turbaveris omnia libidinibus.* Sic igitur, quamvis infideles in suis ritibus peccent, tolerari possunt vel propter aliquod bonum quod ex eis provenit, vel propter aliquod malum quod vitatur." Aquinas, *Summa Theologica*, II–II, q. 10, art. 11, co.

must have the prudence to form all the soldiers to act in common for the sake of victory. In inanimate things, this is seen, for example, in the harmony of notes in a symphony or the harmony of elements in a mixed body. There is some predominate source and orderer of this harmony. The one who has authority in the community should have a special prudence that allows him to judge how each person contributes to the common good and direct that person accordingly. Though justice is important in a ruler, prudence is even more important.

Obviously, any authority must exercise the moral virtues according to what is fitting for the kind of community over which such an authority has charge. Prudence is the director of right reason and so, in particular cases, is absolutely necessary. This is a prerequisite to the execution of justice.

By the same token, those who are subject to authority obey just laws not as slaves or puppets who are moved by a force outside themselves. Whether or not they have participated in the decision, if they understand the truth of the laws, then as free persons, they will embrace such truths as a matter of conscience. A true government does not act on human beings as slaves or through mindless conformity. The true citizen participates in realizing the common good by obedience to the law, which is an exercise of prudence and justice from his point of view. This citizen has dominion over his free acts. So there must be a rectitude in the government and the governed. The rightness of will in the governed is called political prudence, which is the natural response to regnative prudence. This also must implement the ontological good of the powers of human nature.

The rule of a tyrant (one who prefers his private good to the common good) does not bind to rightness of will in those things that are commanded that are sins. The rule of a tyrant is not just because it is not ordered to the true common good but only to a good that is apparent, since it is either the private good of the ruler or contrary to the natural law. Attacking the rule of such a tyrant would not be sedition. "Sedition is a disturbance of the unity of the state in preparation for a physical uprising."[67] Thus, to disturb the rule of a tyrant by resistance, even passive resistance, is not to commit the sin of treason or sedition because that rule is not prudent but rather an exercise of imprudence.

> Tyrannical governments are unjust, opposed to the general good and serving the private good of the ruler. So disturbing such a government is only seditious if the people suffer more from it than the tyrant does. Indeed it is the tyrant who is guilty of sedition, properly speaking, fomenting discord in his people in order to lord it over them more safely. For that is what tyranny is: government for the ruler's personal advantage and the people's harm.[68]

The *Catechism of the Catholic Church* applies this doctrine by setting out conditions for resistance to unjust political authority:

> Armed resistance to oppression by political authority is not legitimate unless all the following conditions are met: 1) there is certain, grave, and prolonged violation

---

[67] "Seditiones sunt tumultus ad pugnam, cum scilicet aliqui se praeparant et intendunt pugnare." Aquinas, *Summa Theologica*, II–II, q. 42, art. 1, co.

[68] "Regimen tyrannicum non est iustum, quia non ordinatur ad bonum commune, sed ad bonum privatum regentis, ut patet per philosophum, in III Polit. et in VIII Ethic. Et ideo perturbatio huius regiminis non habet rationem seditionis, nisi forte quando sic inordinate perturbatur tyranni regimen quod multitudo subiecta maius detrimentum patitur ex perturbatione consequenti quam ex tyranni regimine. Magis autem tyrannus seditiosus est, qui in populo sibi subiecto discordias et seditiones nutrit, ut tutius dominari possit. Hoc enim tyrannicum est, cum sit ordinatum ad bonum proprium praesidentis cum multitudinis nocumento." Aquinas, *Summa Theologica*, II–II, q. 42, art. 2, co.

> of fundamental rights; 2) all other means of redress have
> been exhausted; 3) such resistance will not provoke
> worse disorders; 4) there is well-founded hope of suc-
> cess; and 5) it is impossible reasonably to foresee any
> better solution. (*CCC* 2243)

By implication, such a tyrannous situation can arise even in a democracy if the citizens are motivated by only their own private good against
the common good. Authority is the precedence that one person has
over another coupled with the right to rule the community. Catholic
doctrine holds that the power to rule in the civil and domestic orders
comes from God through the natural order. Thus, it is not just a creation
of the wills of the citizens.

> By "authority" one means the quality by virtue of which
> persons and institutions make laws and give orders to
> men and expect obedience from them.
>
> Every human community needs authority to gov-
> ern it. The foundation of such authority lies in human
> nature....
>
> The authority required by the moral order derives
> from God. (*CCC* 1897–99)

Though authority derives from God, at least the citizens have the right
to determine what sort of government they have and how power will
be given to the authority. "If authority belongs to the order established
by God, 'the choice of the political regime and the appointment of
rulers are left to the free decision of the citizens'" (*CCC* 1901). So
when a statement is made about a given form of authority such as
"Government derives its just powers from the consent of the governed,"
the correct interpretation of this statement is not that the consent of
the governed is the ultimate source of authority. This is God through

secondary causes from the natural or supernatural orders. Rather, it means that the consent of the governed in a civil government decides how this will take place.

> Indeed, very many men of more recent times, walking in the footsteps of those who in a former age assumed to themselves the name of philosophers, say that all power comes from the people; so that those who exercise it in the State do so not as their own, but as delegated to them by the people, and that by this rule, it can be revoked by the will of the very people by whom it was delegated. But from these, Catholics dissent, who affirm that the right to rule is from God, as from a natural and necessary principle. It is important however to remark in this place that those placed over the State may in certain cases be chosen by the will and decision of the multitude, without opposition to or impugning of Catholic doctrine. And by this choice, in truth, the ruler is designated, but the right of ruling is not thereby conferred. Nor is the authority delegated to him, but the person by whom it is exercised is determined.[69]

So the right to exercise the power of ruling in the civil order comes from the type of government the community determines. The precedence of one person over another is not based on an actual superiority but is a moral and juridical one based on the fact that the given authority speaks for the common good as determined by the kind of constitution the State accepts. This also means that the root of authority is in the binding power of the common good and also that laws or commands are restricted by the specific common good of the particular

---

[69] Leo XIII, encyclical letter *Diuturnum Illud*, no. 7.

society. Authority, then, has a true legal and moral right in the moral and juridical order to rule and direct the community that comes not from itself but from the good sought.

The right to have authority in the family, State, and Church confers a true and authentic power. The authority is not just a coordinator with no ability to bind the conscience to actions. Each member of the community also has a true and authentic power that comes from his place in the order of the whole. Since all power and authority is based on the virtues and involved in pursuing the common good, the obligation of members to obey the just laws made by the authority is the same as their obligation to pursue the particular common good involved. If a member refuses to respect the lawful commands of such authorities, he also refuses to respect the common good.

The power of a given authority is limited and restricted. First, it is limited by the fact that the authority exercises such power in the name of God on some level, and so it must conform to the natural or revealed law. Second, such authority is generally restricted to the common good practiced by the community in question and so is also restricted by either natural or revealed law to those goods specific to the community. Human law should express also the restrictions imposed by the type of constitution in a human community. If an authority usurps the function of another community or makes a law contrary to God's law or which is not delegated to him by the constitution, this is not law and therefore does not have to be obeyed.

> We have said that the State must not absorb the individual or the family; both should be allowed free and untrammeled action so far as is consistent with the common good and the interests of others. Nevertheless rulers should be anxious to safeguard the community and its parts; the community, because the conservation

of the community is so emphatically the business of the
supreme power, that the safety of the commonwealth
is not only the first law, but is the government's whole
reason of existence; and its parts, because both philosophy and the Gospel agree in laying down that the
object of the administration of the State should not be
the advantage of the ruler, but the benefit of those over
whom he rules.[70]

Likewise, should an authority command a sin, this is not law and not an
exercise of true power. "Authority is exercised legitimately only when
it seeks the common good of the group concerned and if it employs
morally licit means to attain it. If rulers were to enact unjust laws or
take measures contrary to the moral order, such arrangements would
not be binding in conscience. In such a case, 'authority breaks down
completely and results in shameful abuse'" (CCC 1903).

The primary actions that are subject to human authority in all natural communities are external actions, because man cannot judge the
interior act of the will. As a result, external actions and their relationship
to the common good are the only actions subject to human authority. The community can make use of all moral means to influence the
person toward right conduct. Blackmail, violence, and oppression
would be immoral means.

The obligations of authority, therefore, are (1) to express the
purpose and order of the community for public notice, (2) to ensure
that each member of the community pursues the good according to
the actions that befit his contribution to the common good (3) to
make just laws, (4) to execute the laws in such a way that they are
followed, and (5) to reward lawful actions and punish unlawful ones.

[70] Leo XIII, encyclical letter *Rerum Novarum* (May 15, 1891), no. 28.

These are realized in the family according to the relationship of the parents and children to the act of procreation and education. In the civil order, these are realized by the proper authority established by the citizens according to the form of the individual constitution. Once authority is conferred through birth and the constitution of the State, the authority speaks for God through the natural order if the commands of that authority are just. "The gift of authority is from God, and is, as it were, a participation in the highest of all sovereignties; and it should be exercised as the power of God is exercised — with a fatherly solicitude which not only guides the whole but reaches to details as well."[71]

The Church does not canonize any particular form of government. Monarchy, democracy, oligarchy, or a combination of all three are all in conformity with Catholic doctrine, provided the requirements of authority are met. "There is no question here respecting forms of government, for there is no reason why the Church should not approve of the chief power being held by one man or more, provided only it be just and that it tend to the common advantage."[72]

Respect and obedience is due authority based on the common good, which the authority represents. Such respect and obedience is not due when authority exceeds its competence by commanding something that has nothing to do with the purpose of the society or unjust discrimination among the members or usurps the order reserved to a lower community of a higher authority. For example, if the civil community seeks to declare who is the head of the Church, such a command or law would exceed its competence, since the Church does not belong to the natural, political order but to the supernatural order. The civil order may suggest who occupies such an office, as was

[71] Ibid.
[72] Leo XIII, encyclical letter *Diuturnum Illud*, no. 5.

often the case in Europe, but cannot determine the nature and binding power of such authority, which is established by Christ.

Many people today are very confused about the origin of authority. The denial of objective morals and personal responsibility, coupled with a philosophy of radical individualism that characterizes the twentieth century, has led to a theory of power and authority that is utilitarian. The practical result of this trend is to basically teach that no authority can command unless its command is the result of conclusions reached by a panel of experts who have thoroughly examined the expediency of the given action for attaining the goal. Since there is no real objective truth, life must be guided in all cases by these experts, who also determine morals, again usually by expediency. Democratic vote would determine all truth and morals. A child could have a right to life one day and not have a right to life the next if the consensus of authority changes. There would be no standard outside the consciences of the individuals involved by which they must form their consciences.

The teaching of Vatican II is clear about the origin of authority, repeating what was stated constantly by the popes. "It is clear that the political community and public authority are based on human nature, and therefore that they need to belong to an order established by God; nevertheless, the choice of the political regime and the appointment of rulers are left to the free decision of the citizens."[73]

---

[73] Vatican Council II, pastoral constitution *Gaudium et Spes* (December 7, 1965), no. 74.

FOUR
Authority and Conscience

The Nature and Problem of Conscience

One of the most critical problems in the modern world and the modern Church is the problem of the struggle of the individual conscience in relation to the commands of authority in family, State, and Church. The problem of conscience came to the forefront of moral speculation as a result of the emphasis on the private interpretation of Scripture, which in turn was the fruit of a nominalist view of reality in which one could not know objective truth about things. One only knew one's subjective experience of them. Descartes sought certainty in knowledge but was compromised by a loss of faith in Aristotle when Galileo discovered sunspots and that the stick appearing bent in the water, reason was compromised. The Reformation compromised certainty from the Church and faith. Descartes turned to the "subject" because, when he doubted other authorities, his only certainty was his own doubt.

Fr. Servais Pinckaers emphasizes in his landmark moral study that the casuistic moralists and the manualists saw conscience and its formation as the principal moral problem because of the difficulty in post-Tridentine theology of relating freedom to law. "The treatise on conscience was a creation of casuist morality, which introduced it into fundamental moral theology and hoisted it to the heights."[74] Whereas the moral tradition emanating from the *Summa* of St. Thomas strongly related conscience to the virtue of prudence, in post-Tridentine theology, conscience became "comparable to an intermediate faculty placed between law and freedom."[75] Morality was reduced to case studies to try to determine how much room there was for freedom in the face of the obligations of the law. "The principal task of moralists was to assist conscience in these functions: to inform it of the law and above all to enlighten it in its work of interpreting and applying the law to human acts."[76]

Conscience had always been regarded as the ultimate norm of morality because it was the place where the theoretical moral laws were applied to individual conduct. But due to the denial of the objective nature of the truth about man in the last few centuries in European philosophy, the conscience took on a whole different dimension. Pope St. John Paul II pointed out in *Veritatis Splendor* that the issue of conscience had become so central to morals — and this would include the problem of the relation of conscience to authority — that conscience had taken on the nature of an oracle that alone determined truth. "To the affirmation that one has a duty of follow one's conscience is unduly added the affirmation that one's moral judgment is true merely by the fact that it has its origin in the conscience."[77]

This issue is, of course, also central to the question of freedom in relation to authority. If freedom is based merely on the will's ability to do what the person wants, provided he does not hurt anyone, this includes generally all outside standards and influence. In this view, freedom would basically

---

[74] Servais Pinkaers, *The Sources of Christian Ethics* (Washington, D.C.: Catholic University Press, 1995), 271.

[75] Ibid., 272.

[76] Ibid.

[77] John Paul II, encyclical letter *Veritatis Splendor* (August 6, 1993), no. 32.

be defined as freedom to do what one wants. The conscience would be the only norm for determining such a freedom, and there would be no further standard on which such freedom could be judged. Freedom would be license. Authority in any context would be reduced either to merely a guide to form freedom or a contest of wills to see whose freedom could overpower the other. In society, this basically means that the conscience has rights but no duties. Law is reduced to a struggle of wills.

Many invoke the document in Vatican II about religious liberty of conscience, *Dignitatis Humanae,* to hold that such freedom applies even regarding the commands of the Magisterium within Catholicism so that there is a right to dissent from authority. Yet, Cardinal Newman, one of the most eloquent spokesmen for the liberty of conscience, is clear that "conscience has rights because it has duties."[78] That duty would be to the objective truth with its origin in human nature. This truth in regards to prudence and justice is established in some cases by the lawful prescriptions of authority.

To understand the relationship of conscience to authority, one must first identify the nature of conscience. Conscience is a moral syllogism. That is to say that it is a syllogism in which the major premise, minor premise, and conclusion are an application of the general principles of moral theology to a given individual action that one either has done or proposes to do. It is, therefore, an exercise of the moral truth. The difference between conscience and prudence is that conscience is completed in the judgment of the intellect. Prudence is completed in the action of the will, either acting according to one's conscience or against it.

The major premise in the syllogism is an expression of the general metaphysical relationship of morals to being. Examples would be: "Do good and avoid evil," in reason, or "I must obey the law of God," in revealed religion.

[78] John Henry Newman, *A Letter Addressed to His Grace the Duke of Norfolk: Certain Difficulties Felt by Anglicans in Catholic Teaching* (London: Longman, Green and Company, 1868–1881), 2:250.

The minor premise is a more specific application of this, such as that found in the law of God or the State. Examples would be "Murder is evil" and "Theft is evil."

The conclusion would be an application of these laws to a particular action. An example might be: "This action is murder or theft; therefore, I must not do it."

The binding power of conscience comes from the relation of reason to being. The application of absolute truths in morals to situations is based on the fact that there is an objective human nature that can be generally known through knowledge gained from sense experience. Because God created this nature, the conscience speaks with the voice of God.

> Deep within his conscience man discovers a law which he has not laid upon himself but which he must obey. Its voice, ever calling him to love and to do what is good and to avoid evil, tells him inwardly at the right moment: do this, shun that. For man has in his heart a law inscribed by God. His dignity lies in observing this law, and by it he will be judged. His conscience is man's most secret core and his sanctuary. There he is alone with God whose voice echoes in his depths. By conscience, in a wonderful way, that law is made known which is fulfilled in the love of God and one's own neighbor.[79]

An important source of both the knowledge of objective human nature and the application of that knowledge to practice is the mandate of a given authority in a given community. The closer the good of the community is to the development of the person, the more the mandate of authority on important goods relates to the realization of the human

---

[79] Vatican Council II, pastoral constitution *Gaudium et Spes* (December 7, 1965), no. 16.

soul. Since both the conscience and authority speak with a divine sanction, what happens when the two conflict?

In fact, some Catholics have made much about such a conflict in the contemporary Church and claim a right to dissent from the teachings and laws of authority. There are several problems that need clarification. First, when can someone disobey the commands of authority? Second, under what rubric should one obey a mistaken conscience? Third, what is the difference in the manner in which the commands of authority bind the conscience in the family, the state, and the Church? A special problem concerns the freedom of conscience regarding the practice of religion, which is an important problem in light of Vatican II.

One can only disobey the commands of authority and claim that these commands cannot bind the conscience when such commands are either contrary to the truth or exceed the power of authority. In other words, expediency is not the criterion on which to base the obligation of a subject in conscience to obey the commands of an authority. One is only not obliged when the action commanded is either a sin or is not related to the common good.

> The only reason which men have for not obeying is when anything is demanded of them which is openly repugnant to the natural or the divine law, for it is equally unlawful to command and to do anything in which the law of nature or the will of God is violated.... And yet there is no reason why those who so behave themselves should be accused of refusing obedience; for if the will of the rulers is opposed to the will and laws of God, they themselves exceed the bounds of their own power and pervert justice; nor can their authority then be valid, which, when there is no justice, is null.[80]

[80] Leo XIII, encyclical letter *Diuturnum Illud* (June 29, 1881), no. 15.

In Church matters, one of the reasons that episcopal conferences do not in themselves enjoy the right to teach (*munus docendi*) and so bind the conscience unless given so by the Holy See is that they are not authorities instituted by Christ, such as the bishop and the pope.

Since conscience is a judgment of reason arrived at through the formation of syllogisms, as with all syllogisms, it can be mistaken. In other words, just because a person judges something wrong in his conscience does not mean that it is in fact contrary to the truth. The premises he uses to form his judgment, especially in the minor and the very formation of the syllogism he makes, may be faulty.

Some post-Vatican II theologians questioned this. For one thing, they maintained that conscience was not simply the application of a universal truth to a concrete action. They went so far as to claim there were two systems of ethics: one formed by universal reason, the other by conscience. Rahner, for example, makes a distinction between formal existential ethics and material essential ethics. In his important article "On the Question of a Formal Existential Ethics," reproduced in volume II of his *Theological Investigations*,[81] Karl Rahner introduced a distinction into the moral evaluation of the goodness or evil of actions. This is the distinction between "formal existential ethics" and "material essentialist ethics." According to him, "formal existential ethics" must take account of not only universal norms (laws) but also of the individual historical situation before any true moral analysis of either the good or evil of an action can be considered. This is because each moral act must be something truly personal and unique, and this individuality cannot be expressed in a universal norm. "The concrete moral act is more than just the realization of a universal idea happening here and now in the form

---

[81] Karl Rahner, "On the Question of a Formal Existential Ethics," in *Theological Investigations*, vol. II, trans. Karl H. Kruger (Baltimore: Helicon Press, 1963), 217–34.

of a case. The act is a reality which has a positive and substantial property which is basically and absolutely unique."[82] For Rahner, universal statements like laws can never arrive at expressing personal actions. The basic problem is between the expression of the universal idea and its application to life. "Man is destined to eternal life as an individual and someone in the concrete. His acts are, therefore, not merely of a spatio-temporal kind as is the case with material things; his acts have a meaning for eternity, not only morally but also ontologically."[83]

One must remember that the traditional Thomist solution to the problem of universals is that in every kind of knowledge, though universals are in the mind and not the things, the concept is a true participation in the being of the concrete individual thing. When one knows a real universal idea, in this case the laws, one is truly reflecting what is common in the powers of the human soul in action. The concept or idea is found in the mind and so is spiritual. At the same time, it is a real participation in the being of the thing that it represents and so is an intimate expression of the concrete things, whether material or spiritual. One who has a true concept of a tree participates in the being of all trees, past, present, and future.

The same truth can be applied to man. As in all nature, one understands the powers of a thing by understanding the actions of that thing. When one has a true idea of man because one understands all the powers of the soul and body and their interaction with one another through reason, one truly participates in the being of every man who has existed, does exist, or will exist on earth. This foundational idea is at the root of the formation of human choices in the will because in understanding the universal, one can then guide the further participation in goods in particular. Good adds to truth and being the idea of

[82] Ibid., 225.
[83] Ibid.

desirability. Conclusions about human conduct must result from laws that are universal formulations of those goods that are desirable in various contexts for man based on the nature and relation of his various powers. It is precisely this idea that gives Rahner pause, because it seems to limit the personal encounter of God with each soul.

> It would be absurd for a God-regulated, theological morality to think that God's binding will could only be directed to human action in so far as the latter is simply a realization of the universal norm and universal nature. If the creative will of God is directly and unambiguously directed to the concrete and individual, then surely this is not merely true in so far as this individual reality is the realization of a case of the universal — rather it is directed to the concrete as such, as it really is — to the concrete in its positive, and particularly its substantial, material uniqueness.[84]

For Rahner, God's will is discovered by man in each unique event of his life, in each unique historical situation. No universal idea or norm can adequately deal with the situational complexity of the human person. Yet, if this situation is so unique that no universal laws can be formed about it at all, then this makes all morality merely a fulfillment of the needs of the individual. Morality would be truly the greatest good for the greatest number, with no objective basis. Rahner's solution to this dilemma is to posit two ethical systems that must be observed in every human choice. The first would be the traditional abstract system formed by universal statements in the laws, which is the "material essentialist ethics" already referred to. The second is based on "individual norms"[85] that will complement this

[84] Ibid., 227–28.
[85] Ibid., 228.

traditional system based on abstraction and essences with the existential uniqueness of the individual and is the "formal existential ethics." "The notion of this 'existential' ethics ... shows itself unequivocally as the counter and complementary notion of an abstractly universal 'essentialist' ethics."[86] Each human act has a "non-derivable qualitative property"[87] that cannot be reduced to a norm.

For Rahner, the development of the second science of ethics, formal existential ethics, is necessary for the development of the full complexity of Catholic thought.

> In so far as there is a moral reality in an existential-ethic sense and of a binding kind which nevertheless cannot (in the very nature of things) be translated into universal propositions of material content there must be an existential ethics of a formal kind, i.e. an ethics which treats of the basic elements, the formal structures and the basic manner of perceiving such an existential-ethic reality. Just as, on the one hand, there cannot be any science of the individual considered as a really individual singular as such, and yet, on the other hand, there is a universal formal ontology of individual reality, so (and in this sense) there can and must be a formal doctrine of existential concretion, a formal existential ethics.[88]

Rahner roots this second science in the conscience enlightened by the Holy Spirit using the principles for discernment of spirits found in the *Spiritual Exercises* of St. Ignatius. Until the individual conscience confronts the will of God for the individual manifested by the Holy

---

[86] Ibid., 228, n. 3.
[87] Ibid.
[88] Ibid., 229.

Spirit personally to him, the laws are merely recommendations. The universal laws are partly binding because they are a part of the discernment process. But because of a kind of "supernatural instinct,"[89] the person could always discern that the Holy Spirit was leading him to preserve the basic value taught by the law by breaking its letter.

Since one has formed this existential system of ethics based on an encounter with the Holy Spirit, the implication would be that the judgment of conscience is always a result of the guidance of the Holy Spirit and can never be wrong. In an extreme application of this theory, the judgment the subject arrives at concerning contraception or obedience to the directions of the Holy See about religious life must be followed regardless of its contradiction to the commands of authority. The conscience cannot be false. This is completely contrary not only to the traditional teaching of the Church but to common sense. Since conscience is an application of reason, human reason is fallible and can always be in error. Such an error may be the responsibility of the subject if he has not chosen to inform himself by doing what he could and should do.

If the conscience is correctly formed, there is no moral problem with disobeying the unjust demands of authority. A correct conscience binds substantially in all instances. To change such a conscience would be a sin because it truly reflects reality. If the conscience is mistaken, though, then there is a problem. In the Middle Ages, St. Thomas Aquinas was presented with the dilemma of whether a false conscience could bind a person against the commands of authority. To follow a false conscience leads one to sin against the objective order of the truth. To act against a false conscience leads one to act against what one subjectively perceives to be the truth and so against God also. Some in the Middle Ages maintained that it was not a sin to act against a false conscience, but true to principle St. Thomas maintains that it is.

---

[89] Ibid., 230.

A false conscience does not bind in the same way that a correct one does. It binds accidentally and conditionally. The condition is that if it can be changed, it must be. If one cannot change it, then one is invincibly ignorant, and though the material action performed is a sin, it does not constitute a responsible action, and so one is not held to be culpable for it. However, if it can be changed and one refuses to do it either by omission or commission, then one is responsible for the sin.

The necessity of choice between obedience and conscience is clear in actions that are good or evil in themselves. But in indifferent matters, the principle becomes even clearer. This is despite the fact that St. Thomas expressly states that the conscience binds a person "by virtue of a divine command, either in written law or in the law inherent in our nature. Therefore, to compare the bond of conscience with the bond resulting from the command of a superior is nothing else than to compare the bond of divine command with the bond of superior's command."[90]

The perception that the conscience speaks with the internal command of God is more urgent than even the commands of a superior, and so St. Thomas comes down on the side of conscience in a conflict. However, the distinction between correct and mistaken conscience must be employed. The correct conscience binds "absolutely and perfectly" (*simpliciter et perfecte*),[91] whereas the false conscience only binds "with some qualification and imperfectly" (*secundum quid et imperfecte*).[92] Again, this means that if the subject has it in his power to change his conscience, he must; otherwise he cannot avoid sin. However, when

[90] "Quod conscientia non ligat nisi in vi praecepti divini, vel secundum legem scriptam, vel secundum legem naturae inditi. Comparare igitur ligamen conscientiae ad ligamen quod est ex praecepto praelati, nihil est aliud quam comparare ligamen praecepti divini ad ligamen praecepti praelati." Thomas Aquinas, *De Veritate*, q. 17, art. 5, co.

[91] Ibid.

[92] Ibid.

it comes to the gravity of sin, St. Thomas teaches that the conscience still holds first place because "he sins more if he does not do what his conscience dictates, as long as that conscience remains, since it binds more than the command of the superior."[93]

As to the application of this teaching of legitimate dissent from the Magisterium, it must be stated that the right to freedom of religion declared by the document *Dignitatis Humanae* at Vatican II has to do with the ability of the will to embrace the truth, not to the truth itself. Though many claim this is a change in moral doctrine in which the Church contradicted Her previous teaching on the subject, such is not the case. Leo XIII had already invoked a distinction in *Libertas Praestissimum* (1888) to explain that freedom of religion could be looked on in two ways. One was a result of the rationalists of the eighteenth and nineteenth centuries who declared that human reason can exhaust all truth. By freedom of religion, these thinkers taught that "everyone may, as he chooses, worship God or not."[94] This is condemned because it affects the moral necessity of the intellect to seek truth, especially divine truth.

But Leo also made use of another meaning of the term *liberty of worship*. This could express the fact that "every man in the State may follow the will of God, and, from the consciousness of duty and free from very obstacle, obey his commands. This is true liberty."[95] This is an expression of the freedom of the will in embracing the act of faith. If there is violence done to the will in embracing faith, then this calls the very value of faith embraced into question, because it is not a free human act. In the context of the State, the State cannot as such make any judgments about religion and its truth, as this exceeds its competence.

---

[93] "Magis autem peccat si non faciat, conscientia durante, quod conscientia dictat; cum plus liget quam praeceptum praelati." Ibid.

[94] Leo XIII, encyclical letter *Libertas Praestantissimum* (June 20, 1888), no. 30.

[95] Ibid.

The State could make judgments about whether the practice of a given religion affects the peace and tranquility of its citizens and so limit its practice. For instance, in a State that was overwhelmingly Catholic or Protestant, the State could limit the public expression of religion for peace. If the practices are contrary to the natural law, such as infant sacrifice, it would be within the competence of the State to forbid the practice of that religion altogether.

Despite this power, the Church is clear that an atheist State that sought to limit the Christian faith, for example, would be placing the Church in persecution and should be resisted. The Catholic Faith in no sense can contradict the natural law, and so the State would exceed its competence. The same would be true of any State that sought to determine the nature of offices in the Church. For example, it would exceed the competence of the State to determine that the papacy has no authority over the Catholic Church in a given country and place the sovereign as its head. The same would be true of a State that sought to control all religious practice within a given religion.

Papal teaching up to the time of Vatican II was always trying to defend the freedom of the Church against the state. Vatican II affirms this teaching: "Furthermore, the private and public acts of religion by which men direct themselves to God according to their convictions transcend by their nature the earthly and temporal order of things. Therefore, the civil authority, the purpose of which is the care of the common good in the temporal order, must recognize and look with favor on the religious life of the citizens. But if it presumes to control or restrict religious activity it must be said to have exceeded the limits of its power."[96]

To understand the right of religious freedom that is taught by Vatican II in *Dignitatis Humanae*, one must first recognize that this teaching in no

---

[96] Vatican Council II, Declaration on Religious Freedom *Dignitatis Humanae* (December 7, 1965), no. 3.

sense affects the necessity of Catholics to obey the authority of the Church. The document clearly states: "So while the religious freedom which men demand in fulfilling their obligations to worship God has to do with freedom from coercion [the will] in *civil society*, it leaves intact the traditional Catholic teaching on the moral duty [freedom of intellect] of individuals and societies towards the true religion and the one Church of Christ."[97]

Ever since Vatican II, some Catholics have claimed the right to dissent from a Church teaching that they deem contrary to their conscience. This simply cannot stand, as any Catholic who claims his conscience allows him to dissent from papal teachings has an erroneous conscience, as Vatican II itself makes clear in another place. It is the result of vincible ignorance. This ignorance is a sinful error since it remains within the power of the subject to know the truth and change his conscience to conform to this truth. Vatican II states that such ignorance occurs when a person "takes little trouble to find out what is good and true or when conscience is by degrees almost blinded through the habit of committing sin."[98] The *Catechism of the Catholic Church* states that some causes of this ignorance may be "ignorance of Christ and his Gospel, bad example given by others, enslavement to one's passion, assertion of a mistaken notion of autonomy of conscience, rejection of the Church's authority and her teaching, lack of conversion and of charity" (*CCC* 1792).

Causes of the Mistaken Freedom of Conscience

Though it is true that the conscience is the final place where God speaks to the person about moral life, the judgment of conscience must be constantly verified in relation to reality. The illogical jump from saying that one must always follow one's conscience to saying that there is

[97] Ibid., no. 1.
[98] Vatican Council II, *Gaudium et Spes*, no. 16.

no standard outside the subject leads to the mistaken notion of the autonomy of conscience cited by the *Catechism of the Catholic Church* as the source of erroneous judgments in the conscience. This has led to a spirit in the post-Vatican II Church where many Catholics claim that their lived experience is their only foundation for the truth of their moral conduct and that the authority of the Church is void if it teaches contrary to such an experience.

The origin of this idea is related to a more general mistake in the origin of truth. The source of that error is the philosophy of Enlightenment thinkers. The Enlightenment was characterized by two basic philosophical schools. Following the divorce of sense experience from reason in Descartes, thinkers tended to emphasize either reason or sense experience as the exclusive origin of truth.

The school of Empiricism, characterized by thinkers like David Hume (1711–1776), denied the basic substantial difference between sense knowledge and intellectual knowledge. All knowledge was reduced to the senses and the particular, and the only criteria for truth was that found in sense description. Even ideas like causality were reduced to mere descriptive experience.

Rationalism was a related philosophy that sought to maintain that all truth was found exclusively in human reason. But unlike empiricism, the rationalists maintained that every absolute truth develops independently of sense knowledge. The ideal model for certitude is mathematics, and causality and truth can be reduced to mechanisms. In the nineteenth century, when people accepted the fact that the mechanical view of the world entailed a good deal that was irrational, such as earthquakes and floods and human evil, the mechanical view was changed to an evolutionary one based on progress. The mechanism was perfect as a developing thing obeying its own fixed laws. In nature, this produced "survival of the fittest"; in economics, "the law of supply and demand" as was associated with liberal capitalism.

The common characteristic of both theories is that they deny any objective, universal metaphysical truth that is the origin of truth in the world, either in nature or morals. The human mind is sufficient to know truth either by finding the truth within or by learning the absolutely fixed laws of the mechanisms and learning to manipulate them. In one sense, absolute truth, then, is found in a human reason that creates the truth of the world. The conscience then would only be a perception of a truth man creates himself, and authority would only be one more source of input into this self-fulfilling truth. In the other sense, the truth would only be determined by what allows one to control the mechanism, and so conscience and authority would be reduced to a competition as to which is more powerful.

Since truth is either created by the subject or is merely mechanical manipulation, there is an absolute faith in human goodness. Man cannot be corrupted by sin. Whatever is perceived as sin is really the result of external forces that have not been manipulated properly. Society needs to give as much free reign to the conscience as possible or change the external conditions of society to produce ideal people.

As to religion, every religion that claims to be mediation between God and man is denied. The only real religion is a general one that involves a vague theism and no dogma. The essence of God is completely indefinable, even by analogous or negative knowledge. After creation, God made no more interventions in the world, as it was not necessary. The mechanism would produce perfection if progress were allowed to go on unhindered. All the person needs do is discover the mechanism and use it. The only enduring value of religion was its ability to encourage people to ethical behavior, but there was no supernatural character to it. This understanding of religion easily became atheism.

Since the world is a mechanism, there is no natural law for human beings. All laws are based on materialism and identified with human reason and will to power. The ethical order would be necessary even if God did not exist, but it could not be defined as the same for everyone.

In education, the child is viewed as a moral philosopher in his own right. He must be free to come to the truth with no idea that the teacher actually imparts knowledge to him by active instruction. Instinct alone is sufficient to render the passions reasonable.

In economics, Enlightenment thinkers applied the idea of rationalism to an evolutionary pattern governed also by absolutely fixed, mechanistic laws that had their own logic and perfection. To achieve the perfection of the economy, one simply had to understand what was entailed in the law of supply and demand and apply it to the free market. Promoters of this position were called physiocrats. In the eighteenth century, they applied their theories to emphasize the value of land, self-interest, and lack of interference by others. This eventually became applied in the theory of *laissez-faire*, which maintained that economics was best served when government only supported the right to private property. The unfortunate consequence of this was a lack of emphasis on the corresponding duties of private property and the responsibility that proprietors had for the common good.

In politics, this radical individualism was applied by those who emphasized, on the one hand, the absolute authority of the sovereign and, on the other hand in reaction of the absolute power of kings, the absolute sovereignty of the people to the expense of the natural law and God. Tocqueville expresses this sad fact in *The Old Regime and the French Revolution* when he points out that the monarchy had so identified itself with the nation that no other tradition or institution mattered and could be easily changed by the sovereign. "For some time past the government itself had been busily instilling into the minds of the populace at large what were later to be revolutionary ideas; ideas, that is to say, which taking no account of individuals or private rights, encouraged acts of violence. It was the King who took the lead in showing with what disdain the most venerable and seemingly more firmly established institutions could now be treated."[99]

It was in this climate that Leo XIII and Pius IX condemned freedom of conscience regarding religion. What they were condemning was the corollary notion to the idea that there was no absolute truth apart from the human will or the absolutely fixed evolutionary laws present in nature. This idea was called "indifferentism" because it taught that all religions that encouraged dependence on some sort of impersonal God and philanthropy to others were equally true. Truth in religion was indifferent. The *Syllabus of Errors* condemned religious freedom in this context but not in the context taught by Vatican II, which is freedom of will in embracing the Faith.

Other popes later spoke in the same terms. Pius XII taught tolerance in the light of the totalitarian experience of Fascism and Communism, where the State was all. John XXIII affirmed the rights of a correct conscience. This was, therefore, a homogenous development of the principles that first of all stated that the person had a duty in conscience to seek the one, true Faith. By the same token, the person had a right of freedom from coercion of the will in embracing religious truth. In *Dignitatis Humanae*, freedom of conscience regarding religion is based on two things. One is the dignity of the human person, who has the right to freedom from coercion by the State in embracing the Faith in order to come to the truth freely motivated by a judgment of his intellect. This right affirms the freedom of will necessary for the act of faith. The other is the incompetence of the State to rule in matters that regard truths of the supernatural order, which transcend this world. God may bind the conscience to religious truths through authorities in this world, but this is not done through the civil order but through Christ's Church.

---

[99] Alexis de Tocqueville, *The Old Regime and the French Revolution*, (New York: Knopf Doubleday, 2010) 119.

FIVE

Right

Origin of Rights

Since the beginning of the modern age in the sixteenth century, there has been an increasingly difficult attempt to define the origin of rights. Justice is defined as "the constant and perpetual will to give another his due." The "due" in this case is the "right," which is expressed by *jus* in Latin, a word obviously related to justice.

The question is, what entitles a person to receive rights? In societies that have developed after the denial of metaphysics began with Descartes and his "turn to the subject," the origin of right was in power. There was something subjective about it in the sense that society conferred entitlement to rights on a person.

The ancient idea of right that the Church has made Her own is quite different. The legal entitlement to right follows on the natural right, and the prime origin of natural right is the transcendence of the human soul. The spiritual nature of the human soul sets man above material calculation and so obliges others in justice to recognize this transcendence. In society, the attainment of the common good is very much determined by how much the rights to which a person is entitled as a human are granted and lived. Human beings become debtors as soon as they are born because there are certain rights they must give to others in order to be human. Of course, these are also in some sense based on human calculation. The fact that a person must pay a just price for a service rendered is a part of natural right. What that price is, though, in some sense, is subject to time and place. So, there are three conditions that must be met for a person to be entitled to rights. First, he must be a person; second, to be just, such rights must be observed; third, right, in some sense, realizes equality among human beings. Each receives his own. Only what is strictly due to another can be considered a right.

In societies, rights are recognized and guaranteed by laws. Their origin is either the natural or the positive human law. Natural right is based on those things needed to perfect the human being as such, whether spiritual or material, and is expressed in the natural law. This is a reflection of the idea of man, which is in God's mind and is the source of the objective truth of man. "The natural law is itself the eternal law, implanted in human beings endowed with reason, and inclining them towards their right action and end; it is none other than the eternal reason of the Creator and Ruler of the Universe."[100] Since the natural law is known only by human reason and is not a written law, natural right is not written and the title to it is only founded in human reasoning on human nature.

Human beings are the instruments of guaranteeing natural right by positive right. Positive right can also supplement natural right by conferring title to further goods that are not in themselves necessary to man. Positive right is established by governments. Positive right cannot give title to a right that is contrary to natural right. This would be

[100] Leo XIII, encyclical letter *Libertas Praestantissimum* (June 20, 1888), no. 219.

a usurpation of government. So, might does not make right but serves and furthers it. The current tendency of the nanny state to usurp to itself the ability to determine all rights ignores this obvious truth. This denial is based on the denial of the objective spiritual nature of man. When man is treated only as a material being without a spiritual soul, this leads to determining right only by what is useful. This is contrary to the natural law and natural right and divorces politics from ethics. "Nothing is ever advantageous if at the same time it is not morally good, and it is not because it is useful that it is morally good, but because it is morally good it is also useful."[101]

The tendency to equate political expediency with right was very alive in the 1930s with the totalitarian regimes of the Nazis, Fascists, and Marxists. The tendency to exaggerated socialism today leads to the very real danger that contemporary societies understand the origin of right in the same way.

There is an excellent book written during the Great Depression by Fulton Sheen now again available in print called *Freedom Under God* that addresses this very timely question. In this book, Sheen makes use of the papal social teachings available at that time on a variety of subjects, including the idea that our freedom comes solely from the State. This was a question that was very current because of the ascendancy of Nazism, Fascism, and Marxism, which result from an uncontrolled idea that the State is the sole determiner of rights, justice, and morality.

The State, of course, is a natural society to which all human beings must belong because man is naturally a social animal. However, when the State oversteps its bounds, it does not encourage liberty and freedom but dependence and collectivism. Man is no longer an individual with inalienable rights but a cipher of the collective that must determine and control every facet of his life.

---

[101] Cicero, *De Officiis iii*, 30.

Sheen writes:

> The rights of the person are derived from the good, in
> the sense that every being is directed to that which is
> good. The proximate source of human rights then is not
> the State (Hegel), not the social contract of individual
> wills (Rousseau), not the emergence of new biological
> factors (Spencer), not the will of the majority, not the
> socially useful, not a Constitution, not a Dictator, nor a
> Parliament, but a person made to the image and likeness
> of God, endowed with the power of self-determination
> and therefore the right of self-realization, both in this
> world and in the next.[102]

He then goes on to recount that many think that though the U.S. Constitution was derived from Enlightenment ideas, in fact, it can trace the
emphasis on inalienable right more to Catholic sources, especially a
work of Cardinal Robert Bellarmine, *De Laicis*. The principal theorist
of the divine right of kings, Robert Filmer, wrote a work in which he
disputed Bellarmine. Interestingly, Jefferson had this book in his library,
and the only passage underlined in it is that of Cardinal Bellarmine,
which reads:

> Secular or civil power is instituted by man; it is in the
> people unless they bestow it on a prince. This power is
> immediately in the whole multitude as in the subject
> for it; for this power is in divine law, but the divine law
> has given the power to no particular man.... Power
> is given by the multitude to one man, or to more by
> the same law of nature; for the commonwealth cannot

---

[102] Fulton Sheen, *Freedom Under God*, 148.

exercise this power, therefore it is bound to bestow it upon some one man or some few. It depends upon the consent of the multitude to ordain over themselves a king, or a consul, or other magistrates; and if there be a lawful cause, the multitude may change the kingdom into an aristocracy or a democracy.[103]

Sheen's thesis, reflected by some secular writers of the time, is that this is the origin of the ideal of liberty and inalienable rights in the Declaration of Independence and the Constitution of the United States. He also quotes Washington, who stated: "But let there be no change by usurpation; for though this, in one instance, may be the instrument of good, it is the customary weapon by which free governments are destroyed."[104]

The government of the United States has always recognized many checks and balances in both the rights of the states and individuals to preclude the kind of overarching attempt, even in the name of welfare of the people, to create a government that controls and enters every area of human life: family, education, business, and other areas that no central authority can effectively implement or control. This is to guarantee individual liberties, but it is also based on the recognition that the central government cannot and should not control every aspect of the life of the citizens.

The nanny state is a contemporary expression of the idea that our rights do not have their origin in God or our reasoning souls as individuals, or in any other organ than state control. It is, therefore, morally destructive and cannot be justified.

Rights also confer duties on those who have them. A person who has title to a right may not act according to his title. One may also

[103] Ibid., 152.
[104] Ibid., 153.

abuse rights. "Thus we must be careful not to confuse right with legal usage.... Right is not necessarily lost either by not being used or by misuse.... Thus social grounds as well as considerations for, and necessities of, the common good may require that anyone who misuses his rights or who is not in a condition to use them rationally should be either permanently or temporarily prevented from using them (legal disability)."[105]

Natural Right and Human Right

Natural right is established by the natural law. The term *nature* had a very specialized meaning when used in this context. Natural right cannot be reduced to a merely materialist interpretation, which was favored by nineteenth-century thinkers like Darwin, Feuerbach, and their followers. It is not "survival of the fittest" or "natural selection" or anything of the sort, as this does not take the spiritual soul into account. Also, political thinkers of the Enlightenment who were the pioneers of classical liberalism in the nineteenth century denied metaphysics and the soul, and so their ideas have nothing to do with the natural law taught by the Church. Their ideas also deny the influence of objective truth and God on human conduct. They follow Kant's definition of freedom, which views freedom as lack of external constraint and all law having its origin in the self. Since there are no essences that are not the result of the subjective imposition of man, there is no standard by which to judge or limit freedom. Marx denies natural right and gives complete authority to the collective, which views a human being as a product of impersonal, materialist forces that govern history. Protestants also have a difficulty with the idea of natural right because of the foundational theory of Luther that all that was not grace was sin. Since Protestants

[105] Eberhard Welty, *Man in Society*, vol. 1, *A Handbook of Christian Social Ethics* (Freiberg, West Germany: Herder and Herder, 1960), 196.

have traditionally affirmed the Ten Commandments because they can find them in Scripture, they do in some sense acknowledge natural right. In Islam, there is no natural law and certainly no Ten Commandments. As a result, apart from a few basic imperatives, Islam generally eschews the whole idea of objective right.

The *nature* that is the origin of natural right is identical with God's creation as applied to man. It is thus not identical with natural sciences or with culture, which is what man has made of his nature through external work. Natural right, therefore, includes all that God, in His providence, wills for man, which is based on his being a rational creature with both a spiritual soul and a material body. Both must be taken into account in the assignation of rights. This is enshrined in the natural law.

The natural law contains both general and more specific principles. The general principle is: "Do good and avoid evil." This principle represents the place of the will and its orientation to good in the natural law. The will can only move to pursue a good when guided by the intellect. The intellect is like the eyes; the will is like the feet. The intellect understands a given being in its relationship to the fulfillment of some aspect of the human person, and then based on the hierarchy of powers in man, the will either pursues it or not. For example, for the sake of the truth of the Faith (the intellect), the will could choose not to deny the Faith even though this might lead to the physical evil of death in martyrdom. Or the intellect might present food as desirable because of nutrition, and so the will would desire to eat. Of course, the passions and appetites are also goods of man. A person could just pursue sexuality as pleasant because it feels good. This is fine if the higher goods connected to sex are respected: union of the parties in freedom and procreation and education. But if the pursuit of pleasure leads to denial of these higher goods, then this is an evil that must be avoided. This precept of the natural law connects willing with the objective truth of how various beings truly fulfill man.

The natural law includes those goods that are natural to man. That these are implemented by other goods demands human law. For example, a person may know while driving that he should not kill people. But that this right is guaranteed by traffic ordinances goes beyond merely the natural law and involves human law. Parents have a natural right to control the education of their children. That this may be implemented by free public schooling is human law. The necessity of earning a living and the right to property is a natural right. The worker has a right to determine in which profession he will pursue this right.

The basic goods that are natural to man have been summarized by many people. One example is: "By virtue of his nature man is intended to preserve and protect his life, to procreate; and to prove and perfect himself intellectually and morally both as an individual and social being."[106] The natural human societies to which all men belong, the family and the State exist to promote these goods.

The right to exist includes the necessity of protecting the right of innocent life in the State in all laws and the provision of the family (this includes the economy) to promote this right. This right includes the right to self-defense; the rejection of murder, including abortion; the denial of self-mutilation, sterilization, terror, and undue harsh treatment; the right to earn a living wage and to private property; and the responsibility to ensure just working conditions.

The right to have children entails the right to marry; the duty to guard chastity means that all extramarital sex is a denial of this right; the right to a living wage and to have society guard and ensure hearth and home; the right to education of children includes their physical, moral, and intellectual well-being; the right to be raised by parents and have those parents decide what kind of education is best for their children to be good members of society includes the corresponding

[106] Ibid., 232.

duty of piety and respect of the children to obey and honor their parents. This last right includes the duty also to material support of their parents in their infirmity.

These rights must be guaranteed by the State. They include a solicitude for the freedom of the investigation of the truth and the freedom to discover and practice a religion. The freedom of the Church to promote the Catholic Faith and the public practice of the sacraments flows from this. The right of freedom of speech and association with others is also included. The only basis the State can have for denying these rights is if the association and speech are seditious or contrary to the natural law, such as a religion that would practice infant sacrifice or command the death of the wife with that of the husband.

The right to form the basic natural communities, which are the family and, by extension, business and the State, must be guaranteed. This would include the right of the community to choose which form of government will safeguard these rights and to legislate them according to the constitution chosen by the citizens. The forced taking of children from families for state education, the forced dispersal or enslavement of racial minorities, the denial of rights based on race or religion, ethnic cleansing, or displacement of races would also be contrary to these rights.

People also have a right to form communities that are not natural but respond to certain social needs. These can only be regulated or forbidden if they are contrary to the common good and order of the societies in which they exist. For example, political parties that are founded with the sole aim of destroying the society, labor unions founded to collectivize private property, or terrorist organizations would be examples of communities that are contrary to the natural law. Their purpose is not to ensure the common good of human nature but to destroy it.

These rights are exercised in many different epochs and cultures. Since man in the state of Original Sin is characterized by ignorance, though the most general precepts like doing good and avoiding evil are known by all, practical application of these rights is often mistaken. The ability to know and make good laws was such a rare experience that the ancients often deified lawgivers.

Judeo-Christian thought in this regard has been most helpful because of the divine revelation of the Ten Commandments. Though the Decalogue results from divine revelation to Moses on Mount Sinai, the basic commandments and many of their applications in specific principles can and has been known by some men in most cultures by reason alone. Since they guarantee a correct understanding of human nature, though their application may vary (in Britain to safeguard life people drive on the left-hand side of the road; in the United State they drive on the right-hand side of the road), the principle that there must be standardized traffic laws to ensure safety is inalterable. Such would be the case with all the principles of the natural law. No society may deny them. "In the eyes of the Church these essential rights are so inviolable that no argument of State and no pretext of common good can prevail against them."[107] "But inasmuch as the natural law expresses the dignity of the human person and lays the foundation for his fundamental rights and duties, it is universal in its precepts and its authority extends to all mankind."[108]

Since the natural law is a reflection on the objective human nature created by God, no person or society can dispense from it. The nature of a dispensation is the grant of an authority that has the right to exempt another from following a given law. If someone has a dispensation, he may either not act according to the law or act contrary to it. This is not

---

[107] Pius XII, *Address of September 25, 1949; Christmas Message, 1950.*
[108] John Paul II, encyclical letter *Veritatis Splendor* (August 6, 1993), no. 51.

a sin or evil, because he has been allowed by the competent authority to do so. The only authorities who have the right of dispensation are those who made the law, a higher authority, or someone who has been deputed such a power.

The natural law is instituted by God through the creation of man. No human authority can dispense from it. In the Old Testament, there were examples of dispensations from the natural law derived directly from divine authority: Hosea told to marry a harlot, the Jews told to despoil the Egyptians when they left Egypt, or Abraham told to sacrifice his son. Christ abolished all such dispensations in the New Testament.

Sometimes the question of polygamy in the Old Testament is cited. Two points must be made about this. Though the Old Law permitted polygamy, it is not completely contrary to the natural law, as it affirms the procreative end at the expense of the unitive. Still, John Paul II is clear that this was a result of the devaluation of marriage as a result of the Original Sin. Regarding the permission of divorce by Moses, Christ is also clear that this was a toleration of evil caused by the "hardness of heart" (Matt. 19:8) resulting also from the Original Sin. The Mosaic Law tolerated this practice because otherwise husbands would have sought to rid themselves of an unwelcome marriage by murdering their wives. Also, the prophets are clear that a monogamous, indissoluble marriage is the right one based on the example of Israel's relation to God. Idolatry is often compared by the prophets to polygamy and adultery.

"For there are some who consider themselves morally justified in doing anything, so long as the law of the State allows it or at any rate does not punish it; and even if their conscience forbids it, they will do these things because they have no fear of God and apparently have nothing to fear from the laws of men. And this is attended with disastrous results both to themselves and to many others."[109]

---

[109] Pius XI, encyclical letter *Casti Connubii* (December 31, 1930), no. 131.

Divine Positive Law and Human Law

In addition to the natural law, God has given two other sources for the formation of the conscience in society. The first is revealed law, which is found in the Old and New Testaments.

In the Old Testament, this comprises the Ten Commandments and the specific commands revealed by God for Israel as a holy nation. Thomas Aquinas maintains that the Old Law contains three kinds of precepts: the moral precepts seen in the Ten Commandments in general; the ceremonial precepts, which implement the first three commandments concerning the worship and love of God; and the juridical precepts, which are the last seven commandments and implement the love of neighbor. Christ does not abolish the moral precepts, but He does abolish the specific ceremonial and juridical precepts in the New Testament. The ceremonial laws are fulfilled in His sacrifice and the sacraments, and the juridical precepts are fulfilled in following the example of Christ.

The New Law of Christ is primarily an inner spiritual law by which the Christian is taught the truth by the Holy Spirit. It is not written on tablets of stone as with the Old Law, but on the heart. There are, however, also written precepts that are essentially related to this spiritual law. They either are preparatory to receiving grace, as with the sacraments, or they are essential to living the life of the Holy Spirit within, as with the moral precepts. Though these are few in number compared to the written precepts of Israel, they presume the right intention of divine charity and, therefore, are more difficult to live well.

The New Law is also essential to the formation of conscience. Since its origin is grace, which depends on revelation, its source is equally Scripture and Tradition. Christ founded the Magisterium of the Catholic Church, which is present in both the teaching of the pope and the College of Bishops with the pope as its head to interpret and clarify the

New Law. As this does not contradict the natural law, the Magisterium is also empowered to interpret and clarify the natural law.

In addition to the natural law and revealed law, human beings also make laws for themselves, and this is human law. Civil society is empowered to make specific laws that apply the natural law. However, since human laws bind only insofar as they express human nature and are just, they can never contradict either natural or revealed law. "These human laws which are irreconcilably opposed to the natural law have an innate defect which can be cured neither by compulsion nor by any external display of force."[110]

Epikeia

In the case of human law, there are times when the individual person can claim the law does not apply to him as to its literal interpretation. In certain circumstances, obeying the letter of such a law may lead to a consequence that is precisely contrary to the reason the law was made. This is called *epikeia*, or "equity." Outwardly, this could be interpreted as disobedience. For example, a person is driving on the legal side of the road but a drunk is driving on the wrong side of the road in his direction. If he obeys the letter of the law, both may be killed. In this circumstance, he is not disobeying the spirit of the law but rather obeying it, even though he may be disobeying the letter.

In every human law, there is the letter of the law and then the reason it was made, which is the intention of the lawgiver. The intention of the lawgiver is obviously more important than strict adherence to the letter. "Equity consists in this that the one who is subject to the law dispenses himself from what is demanded of him by the letter of the law. Thus he decides against the letter of the law and in favor of its purpose; against what the lawgiver has formulated, and in favor of what

---

[110] Pius XI, encyclical letter *Mit Brennender Sorge* (March 14, 1937), no. 34.

he intended."[111] The subject takes the responsibility for disobeying the law based on his understanding of what is involved.

Thomas Aquinas says it well: "Legislators concern themselves rather with what is ordinarily the case and formulate laws accordingly. That means that in some cases observance of the law can militate against the equality sought by justice and against the common good at which the law aims.... In some cases it would be wrong to comply with the letter of the law, but right to comply with what justice and the general good require. Equity is the virtue that disposes us to do this."[112]

Equity can be practiced only with regard to human law. One cannot make the same discernment when it is a question of the natural or divine law. Regarding human law, it must be human law strictly speaking that can be defined as a command for which the only sanction comes from human authority. Sometimes human laws only implement the natural or divine law. In this case, there can be no question of equity because the letter cannot contradict justice.

In order for equity to be applied by the individual, the decision must be of great urgency when someone does not have time or ability to consult the legislator and a decision cannot be put off. If the legislator can be contacted for a dispensation, then he must be. Also, though this principle is perfectly valid morally, the subject may still experience some sanction for disobeying the letter of the law.

---

[111] Welty, *Man in Society*, 255.

[112] "Sed legislatores attendunt ad id quod in pluribus accidit, secundum hoc legem ferentes; quam tamen in aliquibus casibus servare est contra aequalitatem iustitiae, et contra bonum commune, quod lex intendit. Sicut lex instituit quod deposita reddantur, quia hoc ut in pluribus iustum est, [...]In his ergo et similibus casibus malum esset sequi legem positam, bonum autem est, praetermissis verbis legis, sequi id quod poscit iustitiae ratio et communis utilitas. Et ad hoc ordinatur epieikeia, quae apud nos dicitur aequitas. Unde patet quod epieikeia est virtus." Aquinas, *Summa Theologica*, II–II, q. 120, co.

No human law can claim responsibility for every choice and decision on the part of the subjects. There are times when the law itself commands something unjust, and in this case, the subject is obliged to disobey in conscience. For instance, during World War II, the Church sometimes falsified baptismal records to save the Jews from concentration camps and death. The Nazi state had no authority to know who was baptized, and since this knowledge would be used to commit mass murder, it would not be contrary to justice for those subject to such laws to simply mislead the authorities. Nor would this be lying, because a lie can only occur against justice when someone has a right to know the truth.

Fundamental Human Rights

Once one has enumerated the various forms of law that make someone the subject of right, it is important to identify the various theories concerning the origin of fundamental human rights that are the backbone of modern states. The history of the United States and Europe is important because of the influence of this history on constitutional law in developing states. A brief history of how societies have codified fundamental rights follows.

The question of fundamental human right is normally thought to have its origin in the *Magna Carta Libertatum*, which the English nobility forced King John I to sign in 1215. The document recognized the freedom of the Church, the freedom of the individual, the freedom of legal trial, protection of widows and orphans, protection of private property, and restriction of taxes owed to the crown. Various English documents expanded these liberties, culminating in the Bill of Rights (1689). England made the transition from an aristocracy to a constitutional monarchy.

During the same period, Englishmen fleeing religious persecution in England came to America and, as one of their first acts, signed the Mayflower Compact. In this document, though they promised fidelity to the king, they also guaranteed equal rights to all the colonists who participated in the common good of the State. This small movement blossomed into the Bill of Rights, which accompanied the United States Constitution in 1791.

In Europe, the movement to enunciate basic human rights began with the French Revolution and the Declaration of the Rights of Man and of the Citizen (1789), which begins with: "All men are born free and with equal rights and they remain so. Differences in social standing can be justified only by virtue of the common good." (Article 1) "These rights are liberty, ownership, security and resistance to oppression." (Article 2) A constitution was approved in France based generally on these rights in 1795, which served as the paradigm for emerging democracies everywhere.

Another experience of the declaration of human rights comes with the Constitution of the Russian Soviet Federated Socialist Republic in 1918. This does away with the right to private ownership in every instance and establishes the collective. The Church is so completely separated from the State that it has no influence on even private education. Only those who work for the collective have the right to vote. The Soviet Constitution of 1936 establishes the right to work, be supported in old age, and generally to equality under the law. The Fascism completely abolished fundamental rights of the individual, as did Nazism: "You are nothing, the people is everything."[113] An attempt to restore fundamental rights was revived with the United Nations Charter. The charter reaffirmed the commitment of the organization to fundamental human rights. In 1948, the United Nations adopted the Universal Declaration of Human Rights.

What is a fundamental right? "A fundamental right is a right which forms the foundation and support for other rights."[114] This is not an interchangeable term with natural right, as it is merely established

---

[113] Welty, *Man in Society*, 264.
[114] Ibid., 265.

constitutionally and perhaps can be changed if the nature of the State is fundamentally altered. A universal human right should be equivalent to natural right, but today the terms are very confused so that basic human rights are thought to be established only by human consent. Though human law may implement fundamental rights in communities, their origin is not the "general will" (Rousseau) of the majority.

The trouble with this point of view is not that it significantly alters certain generally true rights but that God and the natural order are not viewed as their origin. "Important rights are all too easily overlooked (either from want of discernment or purposely for 'tactical reason') and not included in the declaration (because of self-interest; out of consideration for the views of one or the other world-power; or because the defeated nations did not participate)."[115]

The Catholic understanding of these rights is very different. Though human sanction may recognize them, they are promulgated only with the recognition of objective human nature. They are not the same as international law. Since their origin is human nature, they are inviolable and binding regardless of human sanction or agreement. There are also primary fundamental rights and secondary ones. The first relate directly to the goals that perfect human nature. The second derive from these. These latter rights are only valid in certain circumstances. For example, property laws vary greatly from state to state, but the right of property is fundamental. "Primary fundamental rights are: the right to maintain one's life; the right to pursue the ultimate end of life (God and man's own moral perfection) in such wise that it can be obtained; the right to fulfill obligations with personal responsibility; the right to live as a man among fellow-men; the right to marry and to provide for and bring up children; the right to acquire, possess, and use private property."[116]

[115] Ibid., 267.
[116] Ibid., 272.

SIX

Justice and Charity

Nature of Justice

Justice is the central virtue that guarantees Christian social order. It is "the constant and firm will to give their due to God and neighbor" (*CCC* 1807). Justice regarding neighbor is the foundation of Christian social order. The "due" is the right that has already been discussed in a previous chapter. The terms *constant* and *perpetual* designate that justice is not just a sometime thing. One can give another his rights in some things but not in others. Justice is in the will because it involves realizing the good. Justice is more than just a giving of rights. It entails a respect for the other as other. It cannot, therefore, be based on advantage. It is not utilitarian. Justice is concerned only with external things and deeds.

There is a fundamental difference between the modern idea of justice that has it origin in the relativistic philosophy beginning in the eighteenth century, which recognizes no objective nature, and the ancient idea of justice based on the recognition of a prior existing objective nature. Since the modern idea of justice is based only on rights and not normally on duties, justice is primarily about the subject getting his rights. The ancient idea on the other hand is about giving rights to another and so about duties. It is always concerned with the other, not the self. The interior intention of justice is determined by the external act and is so judged. Justice then also has an objective exterior standard that is its measure.

Justice is a virtue that must be developed from the time one reaches the age of reason, because by the very act of being born as a human person, one must restore another in his rights, and so one has duties. This restoration is based on establishing a balance between two parties, and the determination of that balance is founded on what the right is and on the matter in question. This balance is often referred to as "the mean" and is the standard by which both the exterior and interior acts of justice are judged.

Kinds of Justice

There are three kinds of justice: commutative, distributive, and legal. Their distinction is based on the matter involved in determining the mean. The most general kind is legal justice because it is applied to everyone everywhere. This is the justice that is based on the law and entails what the individual owes to the community. Justice between individuals, whether as members of the community or as equals, is divided into distributive justice (community to individual) and com-mutative (individual to individual).

The most basic justice that people practice in everyday life is that between equals, *quid pro quo*, commutative justice. "It belongs to what is called commutative justice, faithfully to respect private ownership, and not to encroach on the rights of another by exceeding the limits of one's own right of property."[117] "Contracts are subject to commuta-

[117] Pius XI, encyclical letter *Quadragesimo Anno* (May 15, 1931), no. 47.

tive justice, which regulates exchanges between persons and between institutions in accordance with a strict respect for their rights. Commutative justice obliges strictly; it requires safeguarding property rights, paying debts, and fulfilling obligations freely contracted. Without commutative justice, no other form of justice is possible" (*CCC* 2411).

The equity between two individuals can be evaluated and judged and does not depend on how the individuals feel about rendering what is due nor on respect of persons. It would be a violation of commutative justice, for example, if a grocer charged one price to his brother and another to a stranger for the same loaf of bread. Material goods basically obey the law of the marketplace. However, this form of justice guarantees an honest day's work and honesty in materials. Higher goods, like art or high fashion, are difficult to evaluate because there is no standard measure for them. Obviously, the falsification of scales in measuring food or other commodities is contrary also to this form of justice. If one has defrauded another in this form of justice or failed to pay what he should, he is bound to restitution. If the goods no longer exist, then he must restore their value. This compensation involves both the good itself and the damage done. One can prosecute another if this happens, and human law is certainly the correct court for making laws about damages incurred either directly or indirectly. The proportion that determines the measure in this justice is arithmetic — that is, what has been taken must be restored according to its value in strict equality, 2/2, 4/4, 6/6.

The second form of justice involving rights given to the individual is distributive justice. This form of justice is on the part of the community for its members and is obviously quite involved in determining social justice. The equity that this form of justice guarantees, unlike commutative justice, is not *quid pro quo* but is determined according to the burdens and contribution of each person to the common good. It would not be just to pay all the same wage for their contribution to a business. For instance, the receptionist in a dentist office does not have an equal burden in providing the service as the hygienist, nor does the hygienist have the same burden or education as the dentist. It is up to the authority in the community to distribute the goods according to the needs and contributions of each. In the case of contracts, of course, a free agent should participate in this decision.

Distributive justice is based on a kind of equality, but it is not that of strict arithmetic equality. Instead, it is a proportionate equality, 2/4, 4/8, 8/16. The graduated income tax, where those with more proportionately pay more, is an example, but how much is paid could be determined, for example, by each person paying the same percentage of his income. "Children in a family are not all given exactly the same food, clothes, education, but rather what is in each case appropriate; which depends on age, sex, state of health, talents, inclinations, even industry. But each child receives what is due to him in relation to others."[118]

This form of justice is objective, even though proportionate, because the proportion must be determined by objective criteria. It may not involve respect of persons. For example, one person may be more qualified than another to fill a teaching position. This is not respect of persons but is based on what is actually the case. However, if an employer were to hire a teacher just because he was his brother, this would be respect of persons. This form of justice must be determined according to the truth of the matter and also must protect the rights of the members of the community to this distribution. One can commit theft secretly by taking the goods of another. One can also commit theft publicly and legally by refusing to pay a just wage or withholding wages. State redistribution of wealth or exaggerated affirmative action that has no relation to the actual people and their needs or gifts would be violations of distributive justice.

[118] Eberhard Welty, *Man in Society*, 301.

This virtue especially applies to judges, who must often determine how to distribute goods and burdens fairly in the community. They are normally bound to judge according to written or common law unless this conflicts with the natural law. In such cases, justice must prevail over the law. Distributive justice is necessary to preserve subsidiarity so that each member of the community enjoys the liberty and rights to which he is entitled. "Hence the preservation of distributive justice offers effective protection against totalitarianism, absolutism in industrial and cultural realms, against unjust taxation."[119]

The final form of justice is legal justice, which entails what the individual owes to the community. This is based on the common good. Since the common good involves the end and order of the community and since it entails a good that normally the individual members could not attain if left to themselves, the community has a right legally to demand certain goods owed by its members. This virtue is called "universal" justice by St. Thomas because it obliges all the members of the community, and the community can demand many works of the other virtues for its maintenance. This virtue is also rooted in both positive and natural law.

This form of justice is implemented by enacted positive laws in society. However, this must always be judged according to the natural law. One cannot say that just because some part of justice is not legally designated that there is no moral or social obligation to pursue it. If a positive law truly commands something necessary for the good of the community according to the natural law, then the member of the community has a serious moral obligation to obey it. If, however, the community imposes unjust laws and very burdensome obligations on the subjects, then the individual is only obliged to do those things truly necessary for distributive justice. For instance, in the example of exposing who is a Christian in

[119] Ibid., 305.

Nazi Germany, which would lead to the death of the Jews, no Christian can be morally obliged to obey this law and it would not be lying or morally evil to falsify baptismal records to save the Jews. The state has no right to know who is or is not a member of the Church, especially when such an evil purpose is involved.

Legal justice, therefore, is necessary to encourage the subjects in a society to actively pursue the common good. This encourages the citizen to truly identify with the community. Laws seek to also encourage the citizens to control their demands and to practice patience when social conditions cannot be altered. The purpose of this virtue is to further peace by establishing an equitable relationship between the common and the private good. The *Catechism of the Catholic Church* summarizes the relation of these three forms of justice: "One distinguishes *commutative* justice from *legal* justice which concerns what the citizen owes in fairness to the community, and from *distributive* justice which regulates what the community owes its citizens in proportion to their contributions and needs" (*CCC* 2411).

Social Justice

The term *social justice*, which is so important in contemporary social order, is of rather recent vintage. The problems of the Industrial Revolution in Europe, plus a new consciousness of developing peoples that occurred with the demise of the great empires after World War Two, brought new urgency to social questions that heretofore had not been so important to moral theology. This was exacerbated by the fact that the twentieth century has witnessed the rise of totalitarianism and more mass murder than any other time in the history of the world. Pius XI reflected on the reaction of the Church to this situation:

> For it is to be noted that besides what is called commutative justice there is also a social justice to be observed,

and this imposes obligations which neither workers
nor employers may evade. It is the function of social
justice to require of each individual that which is necessary for the common good.... The common good of a
society cannot be adequately provided for unless each
individual member, a human being endowed with the
dignity of personality, receives all that he needs to dis-
charge his social function. If social justice is observed,
therefore, the natural economy will bear fruit in the
shape of an intensive and thriving activity, developing
in a peaceful and orderly manner and manifesting the
vigor and stability of the nation.[120]

Social justice is distributive and legal justice combined together. The
formal object of this virtue is still to give another his due. The new and
special nature of this application of these two forms of justice is the
recognition that modern industrialization and globalization, coupled
with the technological revolution provided by the computer, necessitate new expressions of the practical application of justice. These
new circumstances do not cause any variation in the nature of these
two forms of justice. They call forth a new interpretation of how the
various communities relate to each other and how the members adapt
themselves to new social situations. A needed defense of the individual
and subsidiary communities in relationship to the State is always a
challenge. The challenge, then, of the Church is to call all communities
to realize that they are not ends in themselves but must view their laws
as oriented to man as the end. "Her [the Church's] sole purpose has
been care and responsibility for the human person, who has been entrusted to her by Christ himself: for this person, whom, as the Second

---

[120] Pius XI, encyclical letter *Divini Redemptoris* (March 19, 1937), no. 71.

Vatican Council recalls, is the only creature which God willed for its own sake, and for which God has his plan, that is, a share in eternal salvation.... This, and this alone, is the principle which inspires the Church's social doctrine."[121]

Charity

Of course, no treatment of Christian social order would be complete without charity. Charity is the companion virtue to justice. Charity here does not mean love in general or contentment in willing good. In this context, it refers to the supernatural virtue instilled in the Christian by grace by which he experiences a communion of life with God and loves God intimately and his neighbor as himself.

When this is applied to love for mankind, it must be distinguished from affection, the driving force that binds members of a community together, or just the desire to return what is owed in strict justice to others. In this context, it means the very love that Christ has for others and that commands that human beings love others as He did. Charity is applied in action in the corporal and spiritual works of mercy. It is, therefore, the "form of the virtues" (CCC 1827).

Since both justice and charity entail the willing of a good to another, though they differ in object, motive, and obligation, the one presupposes the other. Justice involves strict equality; charity goes beyond strict equality and gives freely as a kind of superabundance. Justice is based on right; charity on love. Justice obliges because of this strict equality; charity obliges because of a common appreciation that all are human beings for whom Christ died and is based on supernatural love. Justice, therefore, has an objective mean; there is no mean in charity.

Still, one cannot have charity without justice. If someone were to give alms and claim that absolved him from paying just wages to

[121] John Paul II, encyclical letter *Centesimus Annus* (May 1, 1991), no. 53.

his workers, this would be immoral on both the counts of justice and charity. "Charity does not deserve the name of charity unless it is grounded in justice.... According to the Apostle, then, all our duties, even those to which we are bound in strict justice, such as the avoidance of murder and theft, are reduced to the one commandment of true charity. It therefore follows that a charity which defrauds the worker of his just wage is no true charity, but a hollow name and a pretense."[122]

Christian charity must affirm the truth of justice but also go beyond it. It must include the "divine pity" for the needs and suffering mankind. It must be guided by discretion and prudence to truly fulfill the wants and needs of men. It would be wrong, for instance, to give someone money freely out of charity when he could work. It would be more charitable to provide him with a job and encourage him to do it. Still, when deeds are necessary, charity requires that they be performed.

[122] Pius XI, *Divini Redemptoris*, no. 49.

SEVEN

The Ten Principles of the Social Order

It is possible to summarize this long analysis of the nature of man in community by giving ten principles for the Christian idea of the social order. I am indebted for a fine book written more than fifty years ago for the identification of these principles: *A Handbook of Christian Social Ethics*.[123] This out-of-print work is a must read for anyone interested in a complete and exhaustive analysis of the traditional ideas of the Catholic Church on social matters.

These ten fundamental principles reflect the kind of society enjoyed by the Persons of the Trinity in God, the archetype of all social union. Social order is one of the principle means God uses to communicate His goodness and glory to creation. The three Persons in God share an infinite nature, and so though They have a marvelous unity in Themselves, They also demonstrate this union in absolute multiplicity. Just as God shows an infinite social union of radically distinct Persons through knowledge and love, so man imitates God in this in society.

[123] Eberhard Welty, A *Handbook of Christian Social Ethics* (Freiberg, West Germany: Herder and Herder, 1960).

All being and all moral actions consist in unity and an order perfected by actions. This order is not an accidental order, as with a heap of stones, but an internal order of action and passion. Participants in society are bound in duty to mirror this union by acting true to their nature and so for a right purpose. Human community does this from the most intimate to the greatest organically. Since the social order reflects the primary society, the Holy Trinity, social life does not find its origin in struggle and strife nor is it just a mere multiplicity joined in a tenuous union but must be a communion that is founded is peace and common agreement. The greater structures like the Church and the State depend on the health of the smaller structures like the family. God could prevent all evil embraced in these structures but would limit many goods and perhaps lead to worse evils in doing so. Each of the ten principles of the social order develops from these principles as from foundation to superstructure. Also, though only Christians could fully understand how these principles reflect the Trinity of Persons, reason can also discover these principles because they reflect the rational nature of man.

Unity

Nature is characterized by a panoply of forms and actions. Yet nature also is witness to a tendency to unity in multiplicity. Each natural being from atoms to solar systems has a diversity of structure that also tends to a unity. Man's social union is the same. The social union is based objectively on his common nature as a reasonable being.

If human beings perceive no common actions that realize their nature together and they proceed from the herd, or crowd, mentality where there is no sense of true union with another, then society is impossible and the human race suffers. Even in the herd, or crowd, mentality, there is little common action as such that results from intelligence and free choice. Crowds are easily moved by mere emotion and propaganda. Many want to reduce political activity to a kind of bipartisan agreement where there is really no disagreement or argument. But this is a peace-at-any-price philosophy that does not allow for the fact that, within the bounds of reason, the loyal opposition exists to provide a check and balance on the herd mentality, to serve unity in action.

The strike, for example, can be a morally legitimate means of correcting the economic order, provided it is not based on class hatred or envy that seeks to destroy those who own property. The aim of the strike should be to force the owners to act like owners and use their goods to serve unity. There is no social structure that is not impaired in its function when unity is lost. This is true of the family, the State, the Church, the parish, the factory, the army, or even a sports team. When people work against each other, the whole purpose of the social union is put in jeopardy.

Order

Social unity is not attained by denying the various contributions, natural talents, and dispositions present in the members of the group. One size does not fit all. Rather, social unity recognizes and encourages the diverse contributions of each member of the group. A symphonic orchestra is composed of a great variety of instruments, and the creation of the symphony does not demand that they all produce the same monotonous sound but respects the contribution of each instrument to the whole piece. Societies that try to destroy classes and different levels of income or outcome for the sake of affirming equality treat democracy as though it was monotony and a system of being as well as a system of government.

Human beings differ greatly in talents, intelligence, and character. Not everyone is capable of speculative thought or is mechanically inclined. It would be illogical to try to put everyone in every job. Social order seeks to respect and encourage the talent of each while also pursuing the common good of all. Also, different societies exist to provide different goods, all of which are necessary for the perfection of man. They are very different from one another. Many of the skills demanded in these societies require a good deal of training or education. The order of a society proceeds in a humane way where each of these goods is affirmed according to the relative contribution. It would, for example, be absurd for the State to claim expertise in economics or medicine and to have bureaucrats making decisions about these spheres who have no training in them.

All totalitarian states seek to deny this just diversity and reduce all to one common denominator. If the totalitarian state is successful, it also creates class envy in which the members of the society not only do not pursue excellence and respect the contribution of each but resent the excellence of others and try to reduce them to the lowest common denominator. "No matter what changes may occur in forms of government, there will ever be differences and inequalities of condition in the State. Society cannot exist or be conceived without them. Some there must be who devote themselves to the work of the commonwealth, who make the laws and administer justice, or whose advice and authority govern the nation in times of peace, and defend it in war."[124]

For this reason, the Church has always considered it immoral to seek to abolish all classes in the State and produce class envy. Social order is not uniformity.

In addition to teaching that the order of society demands a recognition of diversity, the Church also maintains that order must not be based on the destruction of the hierarchy of values in the State in which God comes first. Nor must the values of the State be so arranged

---

[124]Leo XIII, encyclical letter *Rerum Novarum* (May 15, 1891), no. 27.

to put lower values in the place of higher ones. For example, it would be against unity to put race or national honor as the most important value. This would also be true of placing material prosperity in a higher place than moral and spiritual perfection. The same would be true of putting the sciences at the service of racial purity, for example.

If income redistribution means a political philosophy that requires a denial of the right of private property, this is also against the principle of social order. Though private property is not the highest value, still it is an important guarantee of individual freedom, and to forcibly redistribute income against the proper contributions of each person to the economic order is an unjust interference on the part of the State and destructive of social unity. Order would be better assured by the State demanding that those who enjoy the right of private property realize they have a corresponding duty to develop society by providing just goods or services and paying a just wage.

Acting True to Nature

"Every existing community and every social activity actually carried out is always singular and unique; community in general does not exist as such."[125] Man does not exist for the community, but the community exists for man and so must respect human nature. This principle is true in every society. In economics, for instance, the salary is not a commodity to be bought and sold but must be determined according to human nature. The means of production are not the factory implements or the computer but the human soul of the one who operates them.

Nazism maintained that "whatever befits the nation is right," which led to the horrors of Dachau and Auschwitz. Marxism was characterized by situation ethics and reduced human beings to an expediency that did not respect the spiritual nature of man or the natural law. When

[125] Welty, *Man and Society*, 151.

any society reduces law to convention so that it values quick fixes of the moment against more overarching human values, it is impaired deeply. The attempt to solve poverty by contraception and abortion has led to a complete destruction of marriage and even of population to the expense of social taxation and welfare in the Western democracies. Fifty-five million abortions in fifty years have led also to a complete lack of respect for human life.

Acting for a Proper End

Human acts are caused by the pursuit of goals. Even people who commit evil act for the sake of goals that they perceive to be good but are in fact only apparent goods. Acts done in society are also social actions. If a state is to frame laws that are truly human in character, then the purposes they pursue must be in keeping with human nature. They must be moral and good.

There are societies that pursue goals with great zeal and cunning and yet lead to the destruction of human good. Examples would be totalitarian states, Mafia gangs, and unjust business corporations.

For the end of a society to be proper, the ultimate end of human life, God, and His laws must be respected. Any attempt to found an atheistic state must be resisted on the part of both reason and divine law. When God is left out of the picture and His law is not respected, the State substitutes world domination, the pursuit of material goods alone, national or racial purity, victory for the sake of victory, and so forth as the final purposes of the State.

No one may perform or cooperate in an action to further social good contrary to the natural law. So, for example, pursuing, passing, and executing laws that do not defend the life of innocent persons (such as abortion, euthanasia, or execution of prisoners in war) would be gravely contrary to the good of the State. Of course, if a person is invincibly ignorant or committing a crime in a state of passion, he is not morally responsible for such deeds even if they are evil. But as to the evil character, it does not matter if the person who does such things is acting alone or as a member of society.

Morally good intentions or expedient circumstances cannot make an act that is objectively evil a good. One cannot claim that just because one is acting for the good of the nation, the action is good, especially when done under false pretenses. For example, for the Church to take up a national collection labeled as earmarked for the struggle on poverty that actually goes to support community organizing institutions (for example, ACORN) that actively pursue evils contrary to the natural law in a State would be contrary to the natural law. It would be wrong to demand that Church institutions support government programs that espouse abortion or contraception. One might contribute to such collections if one were convinced that his contribution would not contribute to the evil ends or participate in a political party with the express purpose to changing its evil purposes. "Naturally these prospects cannot be calculated beforehand, and hence the justification for taking a risk."[126] As with all human pursuits where danger is involved, there must be a reasonable hope of success.

The Common Good

The common good is both the end and the order necessary to attain the end of a given community. This common good and the order necessary to attain it must be truly good, which means it must accord with the natural law. Because this good leads to a further perfection of man that he could not attain on his own, the community has the right and duty to demand everything necessary to attain this good from its members.

[126] Ibid., 158.

Lest this principle be used to justify totalitarian states, it must be emphasized that the common good must always accord with the moral law. One must also underline that each community has only that competence to demand of its members what truly fits into the common good of that particular society. The State cannot determine the nature of authority in the Church, for example, nor the stamp collecting club what profession its members should choose.

Also, as already noted, human communities can only judge external actions. It would be inappropriate even for the Church to judge the state of a man's soul with regard to God. Even the Church or a religious superior cannot command a manifestation of conscience against the will of the subject. In implementing the common good, the community must be clear about the limitations of what can be demanded and also not attempt to usurp the prerogatives of other communities.

Authority

The authority in the community is the only one deputed to speak for and implement the common good. All communities need authority to direct and encourage the members to pursue the common good of their particular community. Since this is the case, no authority exists to perpetuate or affirm only itself. It is always at the service of the community, given the parameters of the common good.

Mandates by authority, therefore, cannot be pursued that are contrary to justice or no longer expedient to implementing the common good, especially if they militate against it. Each member of the community is a participant in the common good and so has the right to be treated as a human person. If a given person in authority realizes he can no longer exercise his office for a variety of reasons, he has a duty to pass on the authority to someone more suited. This includes training someone who can take his place.

Sins committed by people in authority have a greater weight both in regard to scandal and to leading the community astray. As a result, those who exercise authority are held to a higher standard than other members of the community. A good community must ensure checks and balances on the manner with which authority is exercised. Otherwise, the members of the community will have no ability to defend their rights or obtain redress if their rights are violated. Since obedience is primarily in the intellect and only implemented in the will, truth in practice cannot be just the arbitrary whim or oppressive will of the authority. Modern man would be reduced to a herd. Instead, communities must deal with human beings as persons who are respected as such.

Sometimes, in communities where authority comes from nature — for example, the family — an abuse of authority can only be remedied by the interference of the higher community. In this case, the State has a right to interfere for the good of the victims of the oppressive authority. But it must be emphasized that this is exceptional and only indicated in the circumstances.

Organic Growth

In Catholicism, small is beautiful. Communities develop from smaller and more basic ones, such as the family, to larger ones, such as the State. Nature observes this pattern of growth. If the more basic form of life, the cell, is unhealthy, this can lead to the death of the organism. The same is true of the moral universe. Marriage is the most important community, though the smallest and most basic. From it, family, shop, tribe, state, and Church develop. Those more basic communities are more governed by the natural law because they are more essential to the realization of nature. The health and reform of the larger community depends on that of the more basic.

It would be a social error to try to reform men from the top down. Instead, the role of the larger community is to encourage the reform of the smaller community. The present attempt of the nanny state to make rules for every cell in society — for example, hours of homework or hours of class or medical provisions for a huge nation that are enforced by an army of bureaucrats — can never produce needed stability in education or medicine. The personal dimension is completely removed. The greater community instead must encourage the smallest community to realize the common good that is characteristic of that smaller community on its own level.

Solidarity

The common good that is pursued by the citizens produces a sense in which each belongs to the other. Each is necessary for the perfection of the good, and so each society is complete for the good that it pursues.

This principle means that the society must be able to pursue all that is necessary for its own good. If the State assumes the function of primary educator at the expense of parents, or limits the number of children, the family as a basic unit suffers. Gay marriage attacks the very foundation of marriage as such. In communities determined by the natural law, these ends and means are determined by nature. In those that are the result of only human choice, the scope of the good can be determined by human choice. Since the whole and the part are intimately related to each other, each must depend on the other.

Most communities have drones and queen bees. There are those who freely participate in the good and those who choose to just live off the others. If this happens, then the community cannot attain its full measure. Since everyone in the community has an intellect and will, each person is responsible for fulfilling his part in the pursuit of the common good. Children in families are obliged to obedience and respect; parents to love, care, and educate their children. Employers are morally obliged to pay a just wage and provide humane working conditions; employees are obliged to give an honest day's work. If only the orchestra conductor studies the score, the orchestra cannot play the symphony.

Subsidiarity

This is one of the more important social principles that presupposes all the rest. It is not good for the higher community to try to replace the lower community in the pursuit of the good that is characteristic of the lower community. Each person and each community has a right in justice to proceed according to its own proper place in the order of things. "If the State takes over and claims for itself all the enterprises of private industry, it forgets that those enterprises are regulated by a multiplicity of rules and standards which are peculiar and private to themselves and contribute to the due achievement of their purposes."[127]

The purpose of the higher community is to encourage the lower community to do what it should do on its own. The purpose of the lower community is to act in conjunction with the higher community and carry out the things that it contributes in a timely and responsible way. Thus, subsidiarity must be completed with organic growth and the common good. Also, this principle does not establish what the purpose of the lower community is. This should be determined with discretion by experience and nature. "Nevertheless, it is a fundamental principle of social philosophy, fixed and unchangeable, that one should not withdraw from individuals and commit to the community what they can accomplish by their own enterprise and industry."[128]

---

[127] Pius XII, encyclical letter *Summi Pontificatus* (October 20, 1939), no. 24.
[128] Pius XI, encyclical letter *Quadragesimo Anno* (May 15, 1931), no. 79.

A very practical application of this is that the central government cannot be father, doctor, priest, organizer, and employer for all its members. Nor can the government effectively supplant the initiative of the individual members. Even in a religious community, it would be wrong for the superior to micromanage so that the members are reduced to those who merely obey orders and do not take initiative. Every good superior encourages the members to develop prudence and initiative in their own frame of reference. "The family and society have complimentary functions in defending and fostering the good of each and every human being. But society — more specifically the State — must recognize that 'the family is a society in its own individual right' and so society is under a grave obligation in its relations with the family to adhere to the principle of subsidiarity."[129]

Toleration of Evil

Tolerance is an attitude of soul, a disposition by which one bears evil patiently on account of either avoiding a worse evil or robbing a society of a more central good. But one does not approve of these actions. One tolerates things that one is not able to prohibit or ought not to prohibit for grave reasons. By not resisting these evils, one allows them to exist. One gives comparative permission.

So an authority in a society must occasionally allow the lesser of two evils by comparative permission. At times, this includes tolerating something for the good of peace and security in society that an authority would otherwise forbid. This is political tolerance.

In this, the authority follows the example of God. One important scriptural source for this principle is the parable of the wheat and the tares. Christ states that one must allow the good wheat to grow together with the

---

[129] John Paul II, apostolic exhortation *Familiaris Consortio* (November 22, 1981), no. 45.

weeds because in seeking to root out the weeds, one might also root out some of the good wheat. God will separate them in the next world when judgments about intentions of hearts are clearer. Pius XII gave an excellent description of this principle, and it deserves to be quoted at length:

> Can God, though it would be possible and easy for him to suppress error and moral deviation in some cases, choose to not impede these without contradiction with his own infinite perfection? Can it be the case that in determinate circumstances He does not give to men any mandate to impose any duty, nor give any right to suppress that which is erroneous and false? A glance at reality gives an affirmative answer. It shows that error and sin are found in the world in ample measure. God reproves them, yet he allows them to exist. Thus the affirmation: religious and moral deviation ought always to be impeded, as far as possible, because their tolerance is in itself immoral and cannot be valid absolutely and unconditionally. One the other hand, God has not given any human authority such an absolute and universal warrant either in the field of faith or in that of morals. Such a warrant is not known by the common conviction of men, nor the Christian conscience, nor the fountain of revelation nor the practice of the Church.... The duty to suppress moral and religious deviation cannot thus be an ultimate norm of action. It ought to be subordinated to a higher and more general norm which permits in some circumstances and makes perhaps appear as the better part to not impede error in order to promote a higher good.[130]

[130] Pius XII, *Oratio* (December 6, 1953), AAS, vol. XX (1953), 798 ff.

This principle has an application in many areas of society, especially political society. St. Thomas invoked it, together with a famous quotation of Augustine on prostitution, concerning the toleration of religion. "Human power is derived from divine power and ought to imitate it. But God, although he is omnipotent and the highest good, still permits some evils to happen in the universe, which he could prevent, lest if these were taken away, greater goods would be lost or greater evils would follow. Thus in human authority, those who enjoy precedence rightly tolerate some evils, lest some goods should be impeded or even greater evils incurred. Thus Augustine says in II *De Ordine*, 'Take the prostitutes out of society and you will disturb everything with sexual desire.' "[131]

There are two principles that both must be affirmed in the application of the tolerance of evil, which entails simply choosing not to punish evil, not mandating evil actions as a right. The first is that what is false and evil objectively speaking does not have a right to exist and so to be promoted. The second is that to not impede it by means of state laws and coercive regulations can nevertheless be justified in the interests of a higher and greater good or to avoid a greater evil. One could choose, for example, not to punish a teenage girl who obtained an abortion. One can never say there is a right to choose an abortion. "First and foremost among these is the right to life of every innocent human being. While public authority can sometimes choose not to put a stop to something which — were it prohibited — would cause

---

[131] "Humanum regimen derivatur a divino regimine, et ipsum debet imitari. Deus autem, quamvis sit omnipotens et summe bonus, permittit tamen aliqua mala fieri in universo, quae prohibere posset, ne, eis sublatis, maiora bona tollerentur, vel etiam peiora mala sequerentur. Sic igitur et in regimine humano illi qui praesunt recte aliqua mala tolerant, ne aliqua bona impediantur, vel etiam ne aliqua mala peiora incurrantur, sicut Augustinus dicit, in II de ordine, *aufer meretrices de rebus humanis, turbaveris omnia libidinibus.*" Thomas Aquinas, *Summa Theologica*, II–II, q. 10, art. 11, co.

more serious harm, it can never presume to legitimize as a right of individuals — even if they are the majority of the members of society — an offense against other persons caused by the disregard of so fundamental a right as the right to life."[132]

The first part of the principle is affirmed in the teaching of Pope John Paul II: "In the case of an intrinsically unjust law, such as a law permitting abortion or euthanasia, it is therefore never licit to obey it or to 'take part in a propaganda campaign in favor of such a law, or vote for it.' "[133] One important application of this principle regards voting for laws that limit abortion on demand where there is no hope of passing a law forbidding it altogether. To save many innocent children, a Catholic could vote for such a law in conscience because it is comparative permission. "In a case like the one just mentioned, when it is not possible to overturn or completely abrogate a pro-abortion law, an elected official, whose absolute personal opposition to procured abortion was well known, could licitly support proposals aimed at limiting the harm done by such a law and at lessening its negative consequences at the level of general opinion and public morality. This does not represent an illicit cooperation with an unjust law, but rather a legitimate and proper attempt to limit its evil aspects."[134]

---

[132] John Paul II, encyclical letter *Evangelium Vitae* (March 25, 1995), no. 71.

[133] Congregation for the Doctrine of the Faith, *Declaration on Procured Abortion* (November 18, 1974), no. 22: AAS 66 (1974), 744.

[134] Ibid.

Part 2

Application of Principles to Basic Human Societies

EIGHT

Marriage

Marriage in Divine Providence

The most basic community that is the foundation of all the others is the family. In the moral order, there are several aspects under which the family can be treated. One is from reason under the general order of divine providence. The other is from a personalistic point of view exemplified in the *Theology of the Body* of Pope John Paul II. As this latter perspective includes Sacred Scripture, this is not only from reason but also from faith. Many of the same principles intersect in both treatments.

Marriage is a social institution that is necessary for the perfect realization of divine providence regarding the human race. From the marital relationship ratified in sexuality, God chooses to bring forth mind from matter by direct creation of each and every spiritual soul. The matter in which God has chosen to create this form is the human body, which in turn is generated from the matter of human parents through sexuality. The human soul in turn exists for its perfect act, which is the vision of God in the intellect in Heaven. Through the human soul, the original intention of God in creating the world, which is His glorification through peopling Heaven, can be realized.

In the sacrament of the New Testament established by Christ that is Christian Marriage, this natural relationship receives a deeper and more lasting meaning. One cannot understand this without understanding marriage as it existed before it was a sacrament of the New Testament. The difference between natural marriage and sacramental Marriage is determined by the actual capacity of the soul to attain the ultimate end of Heaven and the relationship of that soul to the Passion of Christ in realizing this final destiny.

In divine providence, which even reason can investigate, the participants in the act by which mind is generated from matter — that is, the procreative act — are not simply two passive participants in an act that is limited to physical sex. Rather, they are co-participants in the action by which God creates the soul. Thus, they are *procreators* since they supply the material of the human body. Catholicism affirms with Aristotle that the soul is the form of the body. There is a substantial unity between the soul and the body in such a deep relationship that the soul can in no way be either a ghost in a machine, as Descartes thought, or merely an unnecessary part of man.

The creation of the human soul in the body supplied by the parents is of such a great dignity that Thomas Aquinas said there was "something divine in human seed."[135] God uses it as a means to bring forth the human soul, which has a potential for an act that goes beyond the material order in intelligence. The procreative act participates in the physical aspects of matter, but from it, a spiritual being issues that will never die. This is seen in the union that man in his person makes of all the powers present in the created universe of which he is a microcosm.

---

[135] "In semine hominis esse quiddam divinum." Thomas Aquinas, *De Malo*, q. 15, art. 2, co.

His physical body is like all physical bodies. If you drop it, it falls. His physical body is also a living body and so shares growth, nutrition, and reproduction with the plants. He also experiences sense knowledge and desire like the animals. His unique action is the spiritual acts of the intellect and will. Man, the person, participates in all these actions of matter and spirit.

Human sexual potential always involves the generation of the human person and thus, as a potency, is never merely a biological function. The being who is generated by means of this power and to which human seed is ordered as a final purpose is always a moral being, since man is a composite of body and spiritual soul. This is why any willed disorder regarding the use of sexual potency never admits of parvity (smallness) of matter but is considered always a mortal sin in object. The good of the propagation of the human race is of such great importance to God because He wants to share His goodness through love, and to do this most effectively, He must people Heaven.

There is a tendency to try to reduce this power to merely a physical action that people use instead of a personal expression of love oriented to human life. But the natural law for human beings always includes a moral dimension, especially if the physical action is oriented to the creation of the human spirit. John Paul II is clear about this in *Veritatis Splendor*: "[The definitions of man as a spiritual and physical being] also remind us that reason and free will are linked with all the bodily and sense faculties.... A doctrine which dissociates the moral act from the bodily dimensions of its exercise is contrary to the teaching of Scripture and Tradition."[136]

Since this act always involves a being that develops beyond matter, the relationship that turns around this act cannot be merely physical or

---

[136] John Paul II, encyclical letter *Veritatis Splendor* (August 6, 1993), nos. 48–49.

material. It also cannot be a creation of human society but is a natural state established by God in the original creation. God is necessarily a part of each sexual act, and so each marriage, because He must create the soul by a direct action of His providence. Of course, since it is a natural moral state, it depends on the consent of the will of the parties to the goods that such a state entails. Vatican II states this truth simply:

> For God himself is the author of marriage and has endowed it with various benefits and with various ends in view; all of these have an important bearing on the continuation of the human race, on the personal development and eternal destiny of every member of the family and on the dignity, stability, peace and prosperity of the family and of the whole human race. By its very nature the institution of marriage and married love is ordered to the procreation and education of offspring and it is in them that it finds is crowning glory. Thus the man and woman who "are no longer two but one", help and serve each other by their marriage partnership; they become conscious of their unity and experience it more deeply from day to day. The intimate union of marriage, as a mutual giving of two persons, and the good of the children demand total fidelity from the spouses and require an unbreakable unity between them.[137]

There are three goods of marriage that must all be protected and encouraged in society, and one cannot be denied for the sake of another. These goods were originally enumerated by St. Augustine, affirmed by Thomas Aquinas and, most recently, in the new *Code of Canon Law*.

[137] Vatican Council II, pastoral constitution *Gaudium et Spes* (December 7, 1965), no. 48.

The marriage covenant, by which a man and a woman
establish between themselves a partnership of their whole
life, and which of its own very nature is ordered to the well-
being of the spouses and to the procreation and education
of children, has, between the baptized been raised by Christ
the Lord to the dignity of a sacrament. (Can. 1055, §1)

The essential properties of marriage are unity and
indissolubility; in Christian marriage they acquire a distinctive firmness by reason of the sacrament. (Can. 1056)

The *Code of Canon Law* seems to downplay the purpose of children in
the text already quoted. Some have said that this shows that the Church
has changed Her teaching on this most important issue.

In fact, the order of enumeration makes no difference to the point.
When Thomas Aquinas discusses this order, he teaches that the good
may be ordered differently depending of what is being emphasized
in marriage, but each is no less essential. This long quote from the
Supplement to the *Summa*[138] makes this point well:

Among the properties of one thing, one is said to be superior to the other because it is more essential or more excellent. Therefore regarding the dignity, the *sacramentum*
(indissolubility) is the most important good of marriage
in all ways than the other goods. This pertains to marriage
as it is a sacrament of grace. The other two pertain to it as
a certain duty of nature. The perfection of grace is more
worthy than the perfection of nature.

---

[138] The *Supplement* to the *Summa* was composed after the death of St.
Thomas by his scribe and friend, Reginald of Piperno. The source
used was St. Thomas's most youthful work, The *Commentary on the
Sentences of Peter Lombard*. It thus does not express his mature thought,
though it is still a useful help to his ideas on many theological matters.

If more principal means more essential then a distinction must be made. For *proles* and *fides* can be considered in two ways. In one way in themselves. Thus they pertain to the use of marriage, by which *proles* are produced and the marriage bond is served. Indissolubility which is meant by sacrament pertains to marriage itself considered in itself. For from the very fact that the parties surrender themselves into the power of the other perpetually by the marriage bond, it follows they cannot separate. Thus marriage is never found without indissolubility, but it is found without *fides* and *proles*, because the essence of a thing does not depend on its use. In this sense, *Sacramentum* is more essential than *fides* and *proles*.

In another way *fides* and *proles* can be considered according to what is in their principles. For *proles*, one means the intention of procreating and for *fides*, the duty to guard faithfulness. Without these marriage cannot exist also. For these are caused in this marriage, from the conjugal bond itself, so that if something contrary to this is expressed in the consent which makes marriage, it would not be a true marriage. Taking *fides* and *proles* thus, *proles* is the most essential in marriage; *fides*, second; and *Sacramentum*, third, as the being of nature is more essential to man than the being of grace, although the being of grace is more worthy.[139]

For the maintenance of the common good of every society, the three goods of marriage must be affirmed: *proles* (procreation and education

---

[139] Thomas Aquinas, *Summa Supplement*, q. 49, art. 3, ad corp.

of children), *fides* (faithfulness and mutual trust and love of the spouses), and *sacramentum* (indissolubility). The present tendencies in Western society so limit the number of children that there is almost zero population growth, and the wholesale contract of no-contest divorce is a serious threat to the peace and stability of civil society. It also compromises the self-esteem and disinterested love of persons in that society for themselves and renders the giving of rights in justice very difficult.

Marriage, when viewed from the metaphysical point of view in divine providence, has a cosmological meaning that enters the moral realm because of the creation of the human soul and the consent of the parties. They consent to share in the creation by God of the human soul as it is generated from the natural receptive potential created from the material union of the spouses.

Because of the widespread practice of divorce, contraception, abortion, and free sex, it seems important to clarify the reasons why marriage is necessary to affirm all these goods for social peace. There are two basic origins of the Church's position, one of which comes from the natural law and the other from a more personalistic contemporary philosophy. St. Thomas treats the traditional natural law arguments in the *Summa Contra Gentiles*, III, 121–129. St. John Paul II treats the personalist case in the *Theology of the Body*, explained in the Wednesday audience discourses he gave from September 5, 1979 until November 28, 1984. It would seem instructive to compare the truths taught first in the traditional explanation and then investigate the same truth in the more contemporary explanation.

Traditional Explanation of the Marriage Covenant

The conjugal bond is established by two persons, man and woman. This is absolutely necessary because of the essential end of procreation and education (*proles*). This relates to the order of providence because it is a participation in the divine action of the creation and implantation of the human soul in a human body. Man has an essentially composite nature of body and soul. He perfects his spiritual self through material and sensible things. Thus, when man improperly uses sensible and material things, his mind is distracted from God, the ordering principle of all his good, and turned to those material things in a disordered way. Material things are a part of human nature, but they are not the highest goods. They are a means to attain the highest goods. Man's mind must be instructed in the proper use of material goods so as to raise his mind to God and to cling to divine law here on earth. He must be centered on God to be perfectly whole, not on things of this earth.

Man's body and his soul belong to God. It is most fitting then that divine providence instruct man in the proper use of earthly goods. They may be used to satisfy human need, but to become a slave to them is to pervert the order of providence. They must be regulated by reason and the divine law. In reason and in the divine law, man is instructed how to make material things, means, or occasions to adhere to God. The commandments given to man in this life, then, are special instructions on the proper use of material things in order to love and cling to God as the final end of man in the order of providence.

Sexuality, which is at the heart of the formation of marriage and the family in exhibiting the relation of two persons with a soul, must respect the order of reason and the objective truth of human nature that is present in the relationship that each thing enjoys to the perfection of the human soul. Affirming the essence of man as a person and so the personal value of the other, one cannot treat sex as simply a biological or material thing that man makes use of as the individual sees fit. Since sexuality is exercised by a being with a spirit and ordered to the existence of other beings with a spirit that transcends matter, it always transcends the material order and must have a moral dimension.

Aquinas expresses this fact well as a truth of faith open to reason alone: "As man's mind is subordinated to God, so is the body subordinated to the soul and the lower powers to reason. But it pertains to divine providence of which the divine law is but a rational plan proposed by God to man, to see that individual things keep their proper order. Therefore, man must be so ordered by the divine law, that his lower powers be subject to reason, and his body to his soul, so that the external things may subserve the needs of man."[140]

John Paul II expresses the same truth in *Familiaris Consortio*:

> Consequently, sexuality, by means of which man and woman give themselves to one another through the acts which are proper and exclusive to spouses, is by no means something purely biological, but concerns the innermost being of the human person as such. It is realized in a truly human way only if it is an integral part of love by which a man and a woman commit themselves totally to one another until death. The total physical self-giving would be a lie if it were not the sign and fruit of a total and personal self-giving, in which the whole person, including the temporal dimension, is present: if the person were to withhold something or reserve the possibility of deciding otherwise in the future, by this very fact he or she would not be giving totally. This

[140] "Sicut autem per corporalia et sensibilia mens hominis elevari potest in Deum, si quis eis in reverentiam Dei debito modo utatur, ita etiam eorum indebitus usus mentem a Deo vel totaliter abstrahit, dum in inferioribus rebus constituitur voluntatis finis; vel mentis intentionem a Deo retardat, dum ultra quam necesse sit, ad huiusmodi res afficimur. Est autem divina lex ad hoc principaliter data ut homo adhaereat Deo. Pertinet igitur ad legem divinam ordinare hominem circa corporalium et sensibilium affectionem et usum." Thomas Aquinas, *Summa Contra Gentiles*, q. 121.

totality required by conjugal love corresponds to the
demands of responsible fertility. This fertility is directed
to the generation of the human being, and so its nature
surpasses the purely biological order and involves a
whole series of personal values.[141]

This unity of the biological and personal order is based on the very
order of the physical act of sharing human semen on the part of the
man in the body of the woman. The personal dimension connected to
this act demonstrates that since the partners participate in a physical
act from which the spiritual soul is generated in providence, the unitive
and procreative must be united. This is strongly affirmed by *Humanae
Vitae*, Vatican II, and *Familiaris Consortio*. The nature of the sexual act
is determined by objective standards that result from a consideration
of how the physical action of the body relates to persons. In the sexual
act, the parents provide the matter, but since the soul can be proven
by reason to transcend matter, only God induces the soul by an act of
direct creation. The sexual action is ordered to this in itself. Though
it resembles acts of animal copulation, since it is physical and some
animals reproduce by sharing of the male seed and the female egg, the
result in the case of man is the human person. The *proles* (offspring)
in itself is rational and so also a person. This fact makes this action
one of the deepest and most personal a human being can do. It also
means that, since the human race is populated by this action, it always
has a social dimension.

Aquinas demonstrates that simple fornication is a mortal sin from
the physical nature of the act presuming this dimension. By simple
fornication, he means any use of the sexual act from which generation
and education of children cannot follow. This is not the result of a

---

[141] John Paul II, apostolic exhortation *Familiaris Consortio* (November
22, 1981), no. 11.

physical defect, as is the case in sterility, but a matter of moral willing. The natural law demonstrates that sex among consenting adults outside marriage is contrary to the very nature of the physical action. In rape, there is no consent; in adultery, the person is bound to another by marriage. Some held that simple fornication when the parties are consenting and bound to no one would only be immoral because of scandal. However, even good actions can be occasions of scandal. In contemporary Western society, such acts as trial marriage or premarital sex are rarely causes of scandal. They may be even be praised.

St. Thomas explains that the only real evil in this act turns around the lack of order in the willed use of the physical semen. Every other thing emitted from the human body, like sweat, perfects the individual. Human seed, which is emitted from the body and physically exists to enter the body of another, contains a life force and so has no individual use. Since the material order serves the spiritual order, one must ask what the truth is about the human seed and its final purpose. This must always transcend the individual good and be ordered to the universal good of the bringing forth of mind from matter, the generation of the human person, the conservation of man as a species, and so the creation of the human soul, which God alone can do. The willed emission and sharing of human seed then must have an order to a good on a more universal level than the individual. It must serve the preparation for human life of another. The sexual act is always ordered to the existence and perfection of another human being.

The physical procreative action becomes a participation in the very creative action of God in making the world. All things come forth from the unity of God and, in their diversity, seek to return to the unity of God — inanimate objects by force of attraction, plants by growth and nutrition, animals by sense knowledge, and man by reason. The bringing forth of human seed is the only action that is ordered to the common good of the human race as a whole. The perfection of this generation does not end in birth but proceeds through life in the perfection of reason and will through moral actions induced by the education of the human being in the virtues and grace. So the emission of human seed has a twofold object: procreation, which is the ontological existence of mind from matter and in matter, and education, which is the final perfection of the human person through the actions of the virtues.

Matrimony, or the right of one human being over another established in the conjugal act, is defined by this action, which necessarily involves a lasting association established between man and woman because of the care necessary to perfect a human soul through education. Unlike the lower animals, formation of a spirit is a delicate task that takes much time, patience, and thought. The proper formation of freedom is no easy matter. Nor is it a matter that can be done in even a few years.

Procreation is the providential means that God has ordained and uses to create man after the creation of Adam and Eve, who were miraculously generated from the matter of the earth. By the formation of education, the human being is instructed so that through free choice, he can participate in the further formation of his soul. As Gregory of Nyssa says, "We are, in a sense, our own parents."[142] Because the body of man is ordered to the perfection of the soul and the soul to God, "there is something divine about human seed."[143]

It follows, then, that it is against the good of the generation of the human race itself that acts should be performed that preclude either the generation of mind from matter or the perfection of the mind so generated. If this inability is the willed result of the individuals performing the acts, their moral participation in this physical act is

[142] Gregory of Nyssa, *The Life of Moses*, 3; SC (1968); PG 44, col. 327b.
[143] "In semine hominis esse quiddam divinum." Thomas Aquinas, *De Malo*, q. 15, art. 2, co.

disordered and has a sinful quality. They are not using these goods as befits a human being with free choice and intelligence, and so their interior wills do not correspond to the justice of God in His divine providence. Since the good involved here is so great, this act cannot admit of parvity of matter. If the inability to have children is due to some physical defect in the body that can in no way be changed by the choice of the participants, this is morally outside the scope of human freedom and comes as a circumstance that is not sinful but that the couple involved must suffer. Such would be the case with sterility.

If however there is no physical defect and the lack of order to procreation and education is the result of human choice, either because the action is done without another person or with a person who is not of the opposite sex, or because the couple take physical steps to prevent the act from participating in divine providence, then the act is disordered with respect to the final purpose of human seed and does not conform to the truth about man, and so is a sin. Such would be the case with bestiality, homosexuality, masturbation, and birth control. It is important to remember that one does not have to have the intention to have a child in every sexual act. The couple may simply have the good of their relationship in mind. But one cannot exclude the ordering of providence to the common good of the human race and the perfection of creation.

One can certainly take pleasure in the sexual act within marriage. There was a long debate about this, and the more rigorist puritanical opinion held that pleasure in sex was a tolerated evil for the sake of the good of children. The opposite opinion was the hedonist opinion that all pleasure is good and one can have sex simply for pleasure without any other good in mind. The Church decided this question and steered a middle course in an allocution of Pius XII. Vatican II approved his teaching:

> "The acts in marriage by which the intimate and chaste
> union of the spouses takes place are noble and honorable;

the truly human performance of these acts fosters the
self-giving they signify and enriches the spouses in joy
and gratitude." Sexuality is a source of joy and pleasure:
"The Creator himself ... established that in the [genera-
tive] function, spouses should experience pleasure and
enjoyment of body and spirit. Therefore, the spouses do
nothing evil in seeking this pleasure and enjoyment. They
accept what the Creator intended for them. At the same
time, spouses know how to keep themselves within the
limits of just moderation." (CCC 2362)

The just moderation spoken of here does not mean just feeling a little
pleasure. It refers to the pleasure the spouses feel as an adjunct experience to preserving the goods of procreation, education, and unity. In
other words, justly moderated pleasure here means using just means.

One may never perform any action that prevents procreation as a
possibility from God because this is a part of the providence by which
God orders the world. Yet, even in an act that is open to the possibilities
of procreation, such as one resulting from natural family planning, this
must still be a truly personal act of love and chastity and not simply a
willed avoidance of birth. This is the procreative aspect and is rooted
in the objective order of creation.

The unitive dimension has a somewhat different aspect, although
it presumes the procreative dimension because the particular kind of
relationship in marriage is specified by this relationship. Since the emission of semen is ordered to the good of the race or the bringing forth
of mind from matter, man must also complete this good by his willed
and social activity. Thus, every act of the emission of semen from which
the proper upbringing of children cannot follow is against the good of
man and also gravely sinful. The upbringing of children demands the
willed participation of both parents to be moral. So the social good of

marriage is based on this aspect of the sharing of semen. Because the human person is such a complex being, the association of the father and mother needed for the education of the child must be long-lasting in nature. Human life is composed of a myriad of goods — physical, sensual, and spiritual — that cannot be easily provided by one person. Generally, the moral commitment of the mother is not in question because the child comes from her body. The moral commitment of the father is another story. Instruction, correction, and affirmation in human children is a lifelong project, though the parental relationship is different at different times. The place of the man and the woman also differ, and the interest and direction of both are necessary for a child to grow up in a mature way. The lifelong commitment of the father and the mother in their consent to live together until death is essential.

In natural marriage, the social relationship that is established by this lifelong commitment determines the nature of the consent that establishes it. The ritual of consent does not matter, provided procreation and education and lifelong exclusive unity between a man and a woman are expressed. Catholics are normally bound to the canonical form of Christian Marriage witnessed by a priest or deacon. The consummation of such a Marriage ratifies the consent so that only God can dissolve it by death. Many Protestants accept civil marriage as Christian Marriage, and this introduces the same obligation. Natural marriage, simply the willed performance of the conjugal act consenting to all that is implied in it, is enough. In this act, man cooperates in the most intimate and powerful way possible to nature in divine providence. If the partners do not consent generally to all it entails — that is, to enjoy the state of marriage — they participate in this act in a disordered and inhuman way.

Sterility is an accidental evil, which is beyond the power of the human will to control, so those who are sterile and yet participate in the marriage act still contract marriage. However, those who are precluded permanently from the performance of the action itself — for example, those who have been castrated — cannot validly give their consent so that the state of marriage can exist. It is the intention to participate in the lifelong relationship that is founded on the sexual act itself that specifies the friendship or mutual relationship of the parties that sets marriage apart from other loving relationships (e.g., friendship, celibate love for God, or affection). The persons encounter each other and give themselves to each other in a context that always relates to the conjugal act.

Marriage, then, is not just a means to have a family. The interpersonal encounter has its own unique experience of the moral good of marriage. The sharing of the semen in the conjugal action is the ratification of the interpersonal relationship already contracted by the parties in the order of providence. This introduces the parties into a common good that goes far beyond the good of their individual selves. In the act, they are man and woman and transcend the people whose names are on their passports. They are partners with God in the creation of a human soul ordered to the good of the race as such and give themselves totally since the human soul transcends matter. In this, they are first of all an image of the manner in which the Persons of the Trinity give Themselves in complete giving and receiving. In the context of the redemption, the further aspect is added to this of the offering of Christ for His body the Church, and so they become priests to one another.

Indissolubility of Marriage

Marriage is, then, naturally indissoluble. Divorce is not just a sin against Christian Marriage but also a sin against the natural law. "The Lord Jesus insisted on the original intention of the Creator who willed that marriage be indissoluble. He abrogates the accommodations that had slipped into the old Law.... Divorce is a grave offense against the natural law.... Divorce is immoral also because it introduces disorder into the family and into society" (*CCC* 2382, 2384–85).

So Marriage is not only indissoluble as a sacrament of the New Law. A corollary to this idea is that though the State may validly contract the civil effects of marriage (property, inheritance, etc.) by registering them, the State does not make marriage but only provides an occasion of consent. Since the consent is the source of the marriage contract because it roots the couple in the providence by which God governs human beings, the State cannot dissolve even a natural marriage. "Divorce is immoral also because it introduces disorder into the family and into society" (*CCC* 2385). Civil divorce is always evil if viewed as the dissolution of anything except the civil effects. However, if civil divorce is merely the dissolution of those civil effects but not viewed as the dissolution of the union as such, then it would not be evil but merely a recognition that insistence on cohabitation and other things of the sort are harmful to one or both of the parties. "The separation of spouses while maintaining the marriage bond can be legitimate in certain cases provided for by canon law. If civil divorce remains the only possible way of ensuring certain legal rights, the care of the children, or the protection of inheritance, it can be tolerated and does not constitute a moral offense" (*CCC* 2383).

This truth is derived by St. Thomas in a metaphysical way from the end of marriage, which is the education of children. The parents must remain with the children a long time for human education in the virtues to take place. Because of the transcendent quality of the person, this is a lifelong commitment. More than one person and one relationship are needed to emotionally and intellectually form a human soul and bring it to maturity. Thus, it is appropriate for man and woman to remain together for a long time even after procreation takes place.

Some psychiatrists maintain that the presence of the mother is essential for education in the primary years because the intellect is not totally formed and the empathy of a woman for the goodness of being is emotionally absolutely necessary for human development. On the other hand, the firm yet compassionate interest and presence of the father is equally necessary in the adolescent years. If either is missing, it is very difficult for some other person to substitute for the parents. This interest based on moral and emotional presences encourages the interest of the parties in one another, too, since they have participated in the formation of souls. It must also be disinterested, because the parent does not take from the child for its own personal need but gives because the parent is an adult. The parents take the place of God in this. God needs nothing from us but gives all.

The interest and commitment to the natural fruit of the sexual act encourages the interest of the spouses in one another. Couples have experienced the fact that when they practice contraception, this creates a climate of use and lack of communication. The personal dimension means nothing, provided that the parties satisfy their desire for pleasure, and so it does not really matter who the partner is in the sexual act. On the other hand, when the couples practice natural family planning, this increases communication and personal interest because it is based on a moral bond. Abstinence for the sake of what is really good and that respects the rights of the Creator in the act does nothing but increase the rooting of the spouses in divine providence.

The qualitative character of the relationship then is based on the good of man as a whole. The final purpose is the generation of human life, which demands personal consent because the participants in the act are human beings, and this, in turn, calls for a long-lasting, indissoluble relationship.

Parental Roles According to Nature

The parents are co-creators of life with God because they provide the material part of the body in which God has chosen to directly create the soul. Marriage serves to bond the man to this life because he does not carry the child physically in his body. Woman has a natural empathy and interest in this life because she carries it in her womb. The father is more tenuously bound to the child. This is because the father does not carry the child, so at times, he must be encouraged to actively participate in the child's life. Of course, there are many men who also have a natural affection and concern for the child that goes very far. For instance, many men are crushed to find out after-the-fact that the child they had helped create was aborted by the woman they loved. Ready to take on all it meant to be a father as well as a husband, this vocation had been stolen from them without their knowledge or consent. They deeply grieved the loss of the child. Such encounters are not uncommon in pastoral ministry. This fact is an important foundation for viewing marriage as a lifetime commitment that encourages a man to be more involved in child-rearing.

The roles of man and woman are different in the education of children. Though their roles are complimentary, their participation is also based on equality. The Nuptial Blessing used in the Marriage rite expresses this well: "May he recognize that she is his equal and an heir with him to the life of grace."

Their roles are also different when it comes to sons and daughters. The role of the father is more one of intellectual affirmation. He must guide the family in truth, especially for adolescents when the intellect becomes very developed. The role of the mother is more one of emotional tenderness and affirmation, which characterizes the primary years when the intellect of the child is either not developed or little developed. Her emotional tenderness begins in the emotional bond she establishes from the time of conception through birth to nurturing.

Both emotional and intellectual affirmation are necessary for the proper education of a child and also must occur over a long period of time. This experience is limited if only one parent participates. St. Thomas says that both parents are needed because human life demands education on many levels: nourishment of body, education of soul to virtue, affectionate experience of the goodness of one's existence, and true correction and formation.

Louis Bouyer gave a slightly different analysis of this same idea in his book *Woman in the Church*. According to him, man is a sacramental representative of the divine action of God in the world. He represents God and the supernatural power of creation in the giving of human life. God's creative power is transferred through man's semen, but man can only represent this force in a limited way because God is infinite and man is finite. The life is generated apart from his in the woman's womb in conception.

Woman represents creation in its high vocation to return to the Creator from Whom it came. In woman, life is brought forth, just as mother earth is the place in which life is brought forth. The movement of creation in its return to God is finally perfected in the reunion of the creature with the first principle from which it sprang. In woman, life is brought forth, just as mother earth is the recipient of the creative force of nature in pagan terms. The life force that begins in material nature is only finally perfected in the union of the creation with the Creator from Whom it sprang. In virginity, a woman is potentially the mother of all the living. She makes this universal motherhood more specific when she brings forth children. In the mother, the divine and human are joined because the human soul is created in her, and this soul is immortal and potentially a place where the union with the divine will take place through grace. As Christ is to His bride the Church, so is the Creator to the earth and the father to the virgin mother.

This mystery is perfectly realized in Mary, who brings forth Him who is both God and man. All women in their virginity are a model of the potential for the divine in creation and, in birth, perform a holy and divine act. The purification of women that was performed in the Old Testament because the woman was considered unclean. She was considered unclean for two reasons. First, she brought forth someone who participated in the Original Sin. But second, she was like the chalice in which the precious Blood is consecrated. Before she could return to ordinary human society, she has to be purified in the same way the altar vessels must be purified to be returned to the cupboard after Mass. In the creation of the human soul in her body, she has come into direct contact with the creative power of God.

Though God, of course, does not have a sex, man represents the divine creative force. But as this is eternal, he can never fully do this. Man is only fully himself when invited by the virgin woman initially to participate in the act of the procreation of the human soul with her on a natural level. Man, as the carrier of the active life force in the semen, is invited into the woman, who becomes a vessel of life and is a preparatory force in which the child is formed and nurtured. Man must then go outside himself to realize his masculinity in its fullness. He must lose himself. Though the male may appear more active in childbearing, he is only the bearer of the life force, not the cause of paternity. This can only formally be God. The man and woman are the material or receptive causes, but the actual reception occurs in the woman herself. The woman is thus stronger psychologically because she can perfectly represent the cosmic forces of creation in union with the Creator. In this sense, Mary represents the Church as the society in which grace is conceived and effects justification and merit. The image of the enclosed garden (*hortus conclusus*) is very apt here.

Since the man represents the divine seed in the order of providence, he is the wise governor in the relationship of the family and the authority who, from his moral strength, creates a safe climate in which the other members of the family can be perfected in an ordered environment. Both husband and wife share the governing of the family, but this is by what Aristotle calls political rule, which means not as master to slave but as wise governor to free citizen. The lifelong relationship of marriage is not the only factor that contributes to this shared responsibility. For this shared responsibility to flourish in raising children and in a complete gift of self to the other, each must exist exclusively for the other, and that other must be of the opposite sex.

If a woman could have more than one husband, as is the case in polyandry, this would deny the role of the male as the wise governor and reduce him to the status of a servant. A man would also be less inclined to have interest in the formation of the children, as he could not be sure which children were his. If a man could have more than one wife, as in polygamy, this would rob the woman of her nature as free citizen in the relationship, deny her equality of freedom with the man, and reduce her to the status of a slave. The woman becomes a tool or object only useful for childbearing in competition with other wives for the interest and affection of her husband. St. Thomas observes: "This argument is corroborated by experience, for among husbands having many wives, the wives have the status like that of servants."[144]

The child is created in the image of God and the likeness also of the parents. The parents must have natural solicitude for the development of their children on every level if they are to assume their proper place in the divine providence of the world. This interest naturally demands the certitude that the child is one's own. The child requires the father's emotional and intellectual interest and direction. This is especially the case in adolescence, when the children are maturing intellectually. Both divorce and polyandry affect this and so are both natural and moral evils.

Marriage, then, demands the participation of both parents, a man and a woman, their different emotional and intellectual perceptions,

---

[144] "Et haec etiam ratio experimento comprobatur: quia apud viros habentes plures uxores, uxores quasi ancillariter habentur." Thomas Aquinas, *Summa Contra Gentiles*, III, q. 124.

with each other in the rearing of children, to truly conform to the natural law for human beings. One must remember that the natural law is not the same as the laws of nature that govern beings that have no reasoning soul. The natural law, rather, refers to the proper interior formation of free choice based on intelligence and will. Since the passions or emotions also participate in this development, a correct formation of the passions in relation to reason is necessary. If either the father or mother does not fulfill his or her role, the family will not easily complete this human formation.

The mother's role based on empathy is demonstrated in her disinterested and loving affirmation of her children in their formative years before puberty. "Woman's vocation is determined by her original vocation of *spouse and mother*. One depends on the other.... It [her soul] is fashioned to be a shelter in which other souls may unfold."[145] The father's role is concerned with developing the correct relationship of ethics to objective truth, and this is primarily developed in adolescence by intellectual affirmation. The father must live and tell the truth. If the child lacks either the emotional affirmation of the mother or the intellectual affirmation of the father, he cannot ethically develop his character well in an ordered way. This affects his perception of both the created order and the spiritual realm of grace.

Many believe that the great threat to family life in the present age is more a problem of authentic fatherhood than motherhood. Again, the father must be morally convinced to interest himself in the integral character development of the children, since they do not come directly from his body. He must be the spiritual head of the family. On the other hand, the mother is more naturally drawn to her children. She is the spiritual heart of the family. In any case, the physical and

---

[145] Edith Stein, *Woman*, vol. 2 (Washington, D.C.: ICS Publications, 1987), 118–19.

spiritual presence of the father is essential as the bedrock for all the other relationships.

Dr. Conrad Baars has expressed this well:

> The role of the father in the prevention of neurosis is not always defined as clearly as that of the mother.... Behind every authentically affirming mother whose tender love gives the infant its feelings of security and happiness, there is a father whose support and protection give her the strength and tranquility of mind to make her love truly creative. Any failure on the part of the husband in this important role will be reflected somehow in the child's growth to maturity through the anxiety caused in its mother.... Homer showed his deep understanding of the nature of woman when, in his famous line in the *Iliad*, he had Andromache bid farewell to her husband, Hector, with the following words, "Hector, you are to me all in one father, venerable mother and brother, you are my husband in the prime of your life."[146]

There is also a natural bond between parents and children that must be respected and encouraged. The parents are the first and most important educators of their children. They enjoy a natural right to both educate and choose the kind of education their children will have without interference from the state. "The fecundity of conjugal love cannot be reduced solely to the procreation of children, but must extend to their moral education and their spiritual formation. 'The role of parents in education is of such important that it is impossible to provide

---

[146] Anna Terrruwe and Conrad W. Baars, *Psychic Wholeness and Healing* (New York: Alba House, 1981), 204–5.

an adequate substitute.' The right and duty of parents to educate their children is primordial and inalienable" (*CCC* 2221).

In both the liberal state and the totalitarian state, such a natural relationship is not respected. In both, marriage and family are looked upon as accidental to the perfection of man. In the liberal model, this is because there is no natural relationship to society; rather, it is simply an accident. In totalitarian states, this is because the state is the only relationship and all others are, therefore, merely incidental and can be sacrificed at the altar of the State. The leader is the ultimate educator and the parents are merely his servants. All experiments in social engineering are based on this mistaken model. In classical liberalism, the State creates the relationship of marriage and family and so can easily dissolve it by civil divorce. The papal encyclicals of the nineteenth and twentieth centuries constantly struggled against any interpretation of marriage and family that would make them simply objects of use for either the emotional satisfaction of the parties or the State. Same-sex marriage is the latest assault of this natural character of the marital union with its rights and duties.

Though one must not completely discount the rights and duties of the State regarding marriage, these are supplemental. According to the principle of subsidiarity, they are primarily about ensuring that the parties who are naturally joined have the freedom and ability to pursue the goods of marriage and family in their own realms.

Since the goods involved in childbirth and child-rearing are so great and transcend the physical order, the relationship embrace concerning them is very deep indeed. Marriage is thus the greatest natural friendship among human beings. The argument based on this deep and abiding friendship, which touches so many intimate goods of the parties and the greatest good of the propagation of the human race, is another for the indissolubility of marriage and also against polygamy.

The greater the friendship, the more solid and long-lasting the relationship will be. In marriage, one finds the greatest natural friendship based on fleshly union and on the whole range of domestic activity that flows from it. The generation of a human being is the only natural act in itself that is ordered to the common good of the whole universe, because the human being that results from it can be joined to God in a union of grace on earth and in a union of ultimate vision in Heaven. Thus, what came forth from unity in diversity can return through diversity to union again with the Creator.

Because the generation of a human being is the only natural act ordered to the common good of the universe, it is rooted in divine providence with laws that are established by the Creator in His very creation of the world. These laws are both natural and divine. The perfection of a human soul is a great undertaking, and the natural law demands that marriage be, therefore, lifelong and so indissoluble. This character is not a creation of human law but based on the ordering of the action to human procreation and education. Divorce is thus a natural evil. It is contrary to this state. "The man they call Paul, did not confine it to *married* couples. Mere copulation, for him makes 'one flesh'.... The truth is that wherever a man lies with a woman, there, whether they like it or not, a transcendental relation is set up between them which must be eternally enjoyed or eternally endured."[147] The possibility of divorce leads to the destruction of family life and thus of society. Some psychiatrists believe that it is a principal contributor to the present prevalence of neurosis in society.

> Whatever detracts from natural family relationships will tend to bring on psychological defects. Foremost among the factors that weaken the natural family bond stands the radical dissolution of marriage: *divorce*. Apart from the emotional shock the child suffers when the father

[147] C. S. Lewis, *The Screwtape Letters* (New York: Macmillan Publishing Company, 1961), 82–83.

and mother, to whom it is tied by the strongest possible
natural bond go their separate ways, it also suffers in its
further development through the lack of a most essential
emotional factor. For only through its relationship with
both parents, not with either the father or the mother
alone, is the child capable of optimal maturation.[148]

One must be clear here that one is not speaking of a civil divorce viewed
as simply dissolving the civil effects of marriage, such as property rights.
One is speaking of the notion that civil divorce can dissolve a valid
marriage bond and thus leave the parties free to marry again.

This natural bond of marriage is strengthened and given a new and
added depth in the sacrament of Christian Marriage because it not
only reflects the union of God with His creation, as will be apparent
in examining Pope John Paul II's *Theology of the Body*, but also adds
the redemptive relation of Christ crucified for love of His Church. As
Christ will never leave His Church even when crucified, the husband
must never leave his wife. Thus, though the union of parents generally
is rooted in the natural order, it is only the generation of children that
specifies the kind of friendship characteristic of Marriage and sets it
apart from other kinds of friendship.

This union affirms the deepest personal relationship in both the
husband and wife, which represents the kind of personal union that
occurs within the Trinity itself. What is affirmed in each of the partners
is the human perfection of the other. Thus, one of the precise aims of
the indissolubility of Marriage is to encourage an undivided union of
giving and receiving love like that which occurs between the Father,
Son, and Holy Spirit in Heaven. This undivided union is implemented
in things like common ownership of goods and peace in society. The

---

[148] Terruwe, *Psychic Wholeness and Healing*, 202–3.

possibility of divorce threatens the very nature of a mature relationship that is expressed by the free choice to live with problems in a relationship that the parties cannot change rather than ending it.

One of the often quoted objections to the indissolubility of marriage is that found in the Gospel passage when Jesus has His conversation with the Pharisees in which He condemns divorce despite the Mosaic Law. Moses permitted divorce not because it was a good but because, if one spouse could not divorce another, they would have dissolved the relationship by murder. To save the innocent spouse, Moses tolerated divorce because of the "hardness of heart" (Matt. 19:8), an expression of the manipulative tendencies that result from concupiscence, would lead to murder. It was still a sin for the party contracting the divorce. Marriage is a natural good, and divorce undermines this good since no one can set aside a Marriage that is valid (*ratum*) and consummated (*consummatum*) except God. Consummation and the valid consent of the parties root this relationship firmly in the common good of the universe governed by divine providence. Only God can release someone from this relationship. A sacramental Marriage adds to this marriage bond a new moral and cosmic dimension in which both the parties as procreators become priests to each other and nurture each other in the special grace of the sacrament. This is the prime example of the priesthood of the laity.

A civil divorce that is viewed as dissolving this relationship itself and thus leaving the parties free to marry someone else is not only a natural evil but also a social evil. Civil divorce is an attack on the natural commitment and indissoluble character of the bond. It attacks the strong and special friendship that is necessary to encourage the further friendship at the basis of civil society. The same is true of extramarital sex and same-sex marriage.

The widespread influence of civil divorce originated in the classical liberalism of the nineteenth century, where society was seen as an accidental creation of the human will and could be easily dispensed with. "But the chief obstacle to the renovation and the rehabilitation of marriage willed by Christ the Redeemer lies ... in the constantly increasing facility of divorce."[149] According to this liberal view, man was not by nature a social animal and mere human choice and human law created the marital relationship. All truths for this philosophy originated in the human intellect, the will, or the sentiments. Marriage became a private contract that could be dissolved either by the State or by the wills of those who embraced it. The connection to the natural order was at best obscure.

The Church has always opposed this liberal view. If divorce only means dissolving the civil effects, such as common ownership of property, then there is no evil. If divorce is looked upon as dissolving a valid marriage bond, then it is against divine, natural, and civil good. Marriage should be indissoluble in both natural and Church law. Marriage is rooted in the order of providence and is not a private contract like other contracts. The civil divorce supports the idea that marriage is solely by the parties together with the State. Civil divorce dissolving a valid Marriage compromises the order of providence and thus all the other goods involved in Marriage. This was foreseen by Leo XIII in the nineteenth century. "Now, since the family and human society at large spring from marriage, these men will on no account allow matrimony to be the subject of the jurisdiction of the Church. Rather, they endeavor to deprive it of all holiness, and so bring it within the contracted sphere of those rights which, having been instituted by man, are ruled and administered by the civil jurisprudence of the community. Wherefore it necessarily follows that they attribute all power over marriage to civil rulers, and allow none whatever to the Church."[150]

[149] Pius XI, encyclical letter *Casti Connubii* (December 31, 193), no. 87.
[150] Leo XIII, encyclical letter *Arcanum Divinae* (February 10, 1880), no. 17.

The Personalist View of John Paul II

The nature of marriage and family has already been treated from a more essentialist point of view, which reflects the natural law. This is not the only manner in which the Catholic doctrine on this subject can be treated, however. It can also be treated from a more personalist perspective, as St. John Paul II has done very ably in both his masterpiece, *Love and Responsibility,* and his Wednesday audience conferences on *Theology of the Body* published in English under the title *Man and Woman He Created Them.*[151]

The teaching on *Theology of the Body* is one of the principal legacies of the pontificate of Pope John Paul II. The pope developed this teaching in his Wednesday audience discourses from September 5, 1979, until February 9, 1983. They are very extensive. Many well-meaning orthodox Catholics have attempted to explain this teaching and its theoretical or practical impact. They have been motivated by the same desire as the pope: to defend the teaching of Paul VI in *Humanae Vitae* in a new, systematic way that takes account of Holy Scripture and sometimes uses a method of exposition derived from twentieth-century phenomenology. Unfortunately, many of the these attempts suffer from a lack of clarity, which has led some people erroneously to conclude that John Paul II's teaching is so revolutionary as to contradict Catholic sexual moral teaching.

Many of these attempts suffer from the fact that they are not based on an adequate understanding of the philosophy and traditional theology that provides the foundation for the pope's thinking. Some want to make him a strict phenomenologist. Others say that, though he takes account of the Scholastic tradition represented by Augustine and Aquinas, he has completely passed beyond that and given a completely

---

[151] John Paul II, *Man and Woman He Created Them* (Boston: Pauline Books and Media, 2006), 735.

new take on the reality of human sexuality. Others go so far as to look on these teachings as a denial of the natural law. Some clarifications of this teaching, then, seem in order.

First, many people seem convinced that Pope John Paul II was not a Thomist but actually accepted phenomenology as the philosophy that most perfectly relates to the present world. The present world, they would say, is no longer enticed by arguments that are objective and deductive but only can relate to arguments that are subjective and inductive. The great proponent of phenomenology is Max Scheler. Scheler's thought was a reaction to Kant's. Both unseated the foundation of a real and objective metaphysics as the correct and perennial philosophy. In a masterful introduction to the new translation of *Theology of the Body* called *Man and Woman He Created Them*, published by the Daughters of St. Paul, Michael Waldstein quotes St. John Paul II: "Due to its phenomenological principles, Scheler's system cannot directly grasp and express that the human person in its acts is the origin of moral good and evil. The whole difficulty is the result of the phenomenological premises of the system and we must assign the blame to these principles."[152] It is obvious from this that though John Paul II may sometimes use the method and language of phenomenology, this presumes an objective and realistic metaphysics derived from sense experience that characterizes Aristotle and St. Thomas.

Second, according to St. John Paul II, the discourses are divided into three parts. One is the examination of marriage based on the words

---

[152] Karol Wojtyła, *Über die Moglichkeit eine Christliche Ethik in Anlehnung an Max Scheler zu schaffen* [Evaluation of the Possibility of Constructing a Christian Ethics on the Assumptions of Mex Scheler's System of Philosophy], ed. Julis Stroynowski, *Primat des Geistes: Philosophische Schriften* (Stuttgart-Degerloch: Seewald, 1980), 115, quoted in John Paul II, *Male and Female He Created Them* (Boston: Pauline Books and Media, 2006), 71.

of Christ. This treatment is in turn divided into three parts: marriage as it existed in Original Justice, marriage as it exists in the state of fallen and redeemed nature, and the spousal meaning of the body as it exists in the next life in Glorified Nature. The second discusses the sacrament of Marriage and is divided into two parts: an examination of the covenant and grace of Marriage and an examination of the sign of Marriage. This is then applied briefly to the teaching of *Humanae Vitae*.

Anyone familiar with the traditional Scholastic analysis of nature as it relates to grace will recognize that the division of the first part of the book perfectly corresponds to the traditional states of human nature as presented by St. Thomas Aquinas. Since this forms the metaphysical foundation for the whole rest of the book, it is obvious that the pope does not deny the philosophy of St. Thomas but rather presupposes it as a marvelous synthesis of the teaching of the Scriptures on the words of Christ. One cannot understand *Theology of the Body* without understand the Scholastic synthesis of these states of human nature. It is this basis that demonstrates that his teaching is not a contradiction but a development of the natural law teaching of St. Thomas already examined.

Pope John Paul II begins his reflections with the question about divorce that the Pharisees asks Christ in Matthew 19:3–8. Our Lord condemns divorce. The Pharisees ask Him why Moses permitted a decree of divorce. The context of the question is the Law of Moses. Christ does not treat the question in light of the Law of Moses but in light of Genesis 2:24. Moses permitted divorce because of the hardness of heart of the human race in the time of Christ. But "in the beginning," it was not so. One must then examine marriage from the standpoint of nature as God intended it.

The traditional Scholastic teaching canonized by the Council of Trent taught that man was created in grace and that he was endowed man objectively with special gifts called preternatural gifts. Here is part of a footnote about the state of integrity, or Original Justice, in which the pope himself uses the terms: " 'Even if human nature had remained *in the integrity in which it was created,* it could not at all have kept this integrity without the help of the Creator' (DS 389).... 'The first man was also free from the necessity of death' (DS 222, 372, 1511). 'The Council of Trent defines the state of the first man before sin as "holiness and justice" (DS 1511, 1512) or as "innocence" (DS 1521).' "[153] The general division of the theoretical part of *Theology of the Body* perfectly reflects the traditional division of the states of nature of which this is the first part. They are: the state of Original Justice, or Integrity (discourses 1–23); the state of fallen and redeemed nature (discourses 24–63); and the state of Glorified Nature (discourses 64–86). This forms about half of the teaching (133 discourses). It is important to understand the main themes in each section.

Section one examines the conjugal relationship in the state of Original Justice. There are several themes: original solitude, the original unity of man and woman, and original nakedness. The *leitmotif* under them all is the spousal meaning of the body. John Paul II states that Christ wants to go back to "in the beginning" to examine the human nature of the conjugal relationship. He first discusses Genesis 1 and explains that this is an objective and essentialist treatment of the issue. In fact, the first three chapters of Genesis are "myth," but after rejecting many definitions of this word, he gives his own. Myth, in the sense Genesis uses it, expresses " '*in nucleo*' almost all the elements of the analysis of man to which modern, and above all contemporary, philosophical anthropology is sensitive."[154] It is thus more or less a primitive way of expressing philosophical truth that does not take account of the vocabulary of traditional philosophy. In this first chapter, man is described as different from the rest of creation, made in His image both male and female. Man and woman, made in God's image, are to increase and multiply.

[153] John Paul II, *Male and Female He Created Them,* 239, n. 44.
[154] Ibid., 138.

The second chapter of Genesis, which is older than the first chronologically, represents the same truths but includes the human subjective reactions to such truths. First, human beings are stated to be different from the rest of creation in the original solitude. They have a mind, because Adam knows all the animals on first experience, and a will, because they are invited to be partners with God in realizing their destiny through human choice. Man names all the animals and finds none like him, and so he is alone. This is original solitude. God declares, "It is not good for man to be alone" (Gen. 2:18). Why? Because God is not alone but a communion of Persons Who spend all eternity giving and receiving. This is the great truth expressed in the traditional teaching of the Trinity on *perichoresis* and *circumincession*. God is a society in which all is gift and reception in truth and love. If man is to be made fully in God's image, he must be finally created with the possibility of interpersonal union. Hence, the creation of Eve.

When Adam sees Eve, he finds one like himself, the first great cry of joy is given in the history of the human race, and he names her: "This at last is bone of my bones and flesh of my flesh, she shall be called woman as she has been taken out of man" (Gen. 2:23). This recognition is made not only with the soul but also through the body. The two become one flesh. Their gift and reception of soul is expressed through the body because man is not just a soul but a composite of body and soul. This is called the spousal meaning of the body because the body itself is a vehicle that expresses the freedom of giving in the soul. The body participates in the giving of the soul because, according to Vatican II,[155] persons must be ethically treated in two ways: (1) no person may be an object of use, but every person must be a subject of love; (2) a person only finds himself in a sincere gift of himself.

Man experiences this spousal meaning of the body as a reflection of the life of the Trinity. So Marriage, in the beginning, is a reflection

---

[155] Vatican Council II, *Gaudium et Spes*, no. 24.

of the Trinity and also of God giving life, a fruit of this spiritual union. Already, the three great goods of Marriage — fidelity, friendship, and fertility — are present in this text. Adam and Eve experience this spontaneously because, since they are full of grace, they have a gift from God infused at creation in which their passions perfectly express this spousal meaning. They are "naked and not ashamed" (Gen. 2:25). Shame is caused in the phenomenological sense by the possibility of the gift of self being exploited by another against the will of the giver, by the experience of domination instead of gift. Because of the presence of grace, this was not possible for Adam and Eve as long as they lived in the grace of God. They had an easy virtue. This is the original nakedness.

Anyone familiar with the natural, preternatural, and supernatural gifts of Scholastic theology will recognize them in this presentation. The natural gifts are the faculties of man: intellect, will, passions, and body. All are ontologically good. The supernatural gift is the grace of God in which both of our first parents were created. The preternatural gifts are seen in Adam's infused knowledge of the animals, his easy obedience, and the easy virtue of governing his passions in sexuality coupled with his lack of the experience of death. The only innovation in this teaching of the pope's is deriving these same truths from the subjective experience of man using Genesis 2.

The same spousal love is underneath the explanation John Paul II gives of the next great state of human nature: fallen and redeemed nature. The basic experience of this state is described in Genesis 3, and the pope calls this original shame. Adam and Eve questioned the fact that grace was a gift. They did not do this intellectually but rather morally. The pope says that it is as a result of this question that a completely different experience of man/woman relations arises characterized objectively by the loss of grace. The loss of grace causes shame at the presence of the body not because it is evil but because it moves from being a vehicle of gift to having a very real potential for the egotistical extortion of the gift of self. God says to the woman: "Your desire shall be for your husband and he shall rule over you" (Gen. 3:16). Man extorts from woman through strength and woman extorts from man by trickery. Neither one is motivated by giving the gift of self but by taking the self of the other against the other's will.

This shame is expressed in the threefold concupiscence, or lust, described in 1 John 2:16: the lust of the flesh, the lust of the eyes, and the pride of life. Our experience of egotistically trying to dominate is what characterizes the state that we experience now, or what the pope calls the historical experience of man/woman relationships now. Again, John Paul II uses classic terminology, calling this "the 'state' of 'historical' man as *status naturae lapsae simul ac redemptae* [the state of fallen and at the same time redeemed nature] (*MTW*, 308)."[156]

The experience of the original shame is expressed by Jesus as "the lustful look" (Matt. 5:28). A classic example of the "lustful look" is found in the story of the look of David on Bathsheba (2 Sam. 11:2), a look that led him to such hardness of heart (cf. Matt. 19:8) that David sought to cover his sin by the death of the innocent Uriah, her husband. Yet, this teaching of Christ is not an indictment of the body as evil but an accusation of the human heart that uses the body to dominate another. But "this statement [of] the human 'heart' is above all the object of a call and not of an accusation."[157] "*In the Bible the threefold concupiscence does not constitute the fundamental* and certainly the only and absolute *criterion* of anthropology and ethics, although it is without doubt *an important coefficient for understanding man.*"[158] This is not a Manichean attitude where the body is looked on as evil, but rather the body used as a vehicle for egotism is "a value not sufficiently appreciated."[159]

[156] John Paul II, *Male and Female He Created Them*, 308.
[157] Ibid., 325.
[158] Ibid.
[159] Ibid., 307.

The fullness of the experience of the body in the second state then requires that it be redeemed and returned to its rightful place as a vehicle of the communion of persons. Grace allows this to happen. "We know that the whole creation has been groaning in travail together until now, and not only the creation, but we ourselves who have the first fruits of the Spirit groan inwardly as we wait for adoption as sons, the redemption of our bodies" (Rom. 8:22–23). That very redemption requires returning human experience by the healing of grace to a union again of eros (the body and passions) with ethos (the love of the will). This is done through the classic virtue of temperance using self-restraint born of love. Again, this merely reflects the classic teaching of St. Thomas. "In themselves passions are neither good nor evil. They are morally qualified only to the extent that they effectively engage reason and will.... It belongs to the perfection of the moral or human good that the passions be governed by reason" (CCC 1767).

The third great experience in the "triptych" of human experience concerning sexuality is found in the state of Glorified Nature, which Christ references in His conversation with the Sadducees about the resurrection of the dead (see Mark 12:18–27). This is the state where "they neither marry nor are given in marriage." Instead, in this state, there is a new relation between body and spirit other than the one in this life. St. Paul describes this relationship in 1 Corinthians. "The first Adam became a living being; the last Adam became a life-giving spirit.... The first man was born from the earth, a man of dust; the second man is from heaven.... Just as we have borne the man of dust, we shall also bear the image of the man from heaven."[160] This new relationship completes the revelation of the body. Once we see God face-to-face, this leads to a new psychosomatic experience of the gift of self that is characterized by virginity. Every soul is virginal in Heaven, and the

---

[160] Ibid., 45–50.

body reflects this because God fills every faculty beginning with the intellect. Pope John Paul II says this leads to a *restitutio in integrum* (a restoring of integrity) that is experienced not only in the soul but in the joy of all the senses. Again, the pope expresses the doctrine of St. Thomas: "When St. Thomas in his anthropology accepted Aristotle's conception [as opposed to Plato's idea of the relation of the soul and the body], he did so because he considered the truth about the resurrection. In fact, the truth about the resurrection clearly affirms that man's eschatological perfection and happiness cannot be understood as a state of the soul alone, separated (according to Plato, liberated) from the body, but must be understood as *the definitively and perfectly 'integrated' state of man* brought about by such a union of the soul with the body that it definitively qualifies and assures this perfect integrity."[161] Man, however, now is " 'set in tension' between these two poles *in the perspective of eternal destiny* that concerns from the beginning to the end his same human nature."[162]

Virginity is in no sense a denial of the spousal meaning of the body, as though the body were evil, but rather an affirmation of that spousal meaning in the way it will exist in Heaven, which in terms of this earth must be looked upon as exceptional, a recommendation of Christ. He returns to the original text about divorce here. "Not all men can receive this precept, but only those to whom it is given. For there are eunuchs who have been so from birth, eunuchs who have been made eunuchs by men and eunuchs who have made themselves so for the sake of the kingdom of heaven. He who is able to receive this, let him receive it" (Matt. 19:11–12). This involves a renunciation of Marriage but not the values of Marriage nor of the spousal meaning of the body. "If someone chooses marriage, he must choose it exactly

[161] Ibid., 390.
[162] Ibid., 406.

as it was instituted by the Creator 'from the beginning'; ... if on the other hand someone decides to follow continence for the kingdom of heaven, he must seek in it the values proper to such a vocation."[163] Again, this reflects common Church doctrine, " 'Whoever denigrates marriage also diminishes the glory of virginity' " (CCC 1620).

The pope then applies this whole doctrine of man to the relationship of Marriage as expressed in both Ephesians 5:22–33 and the Song of Songs. The key concepts here are Marriage as the great sacrament and what he calls the prophetism of the body. He wishes to highlight that for St. Paul in Ephesians, Christ seeks to recover the same value of Marriage as spousal man experienced before the Fall but now also expressing His relationship with His Church, which is shown in His willingness to die for His Church. "*The institution of marriage* according to the words of Genesis 2:24, expresses not only the beginning of the fundamental human community, which by the 'procreative' power proper to it ('be fruitful and multiply,' Gen. 1:28) serves to continue the work of creation, but at the same time *it expresses the Creator's salvific initiative*, which corresponds to man's eternal election spoken about in Ephesians."[164]

The grace of Marriage allows the parties to become one flesh just as Christ is one with His bride the Church, and calls forth from them the same love Christ has for His Church, a love of spouse for bride endowed with all the rich teaching of the covenant and prophets in the Old Testament, but fulfilled by Christ.

This union is expressed when the parties speak works in their bodies which express their communion of souls in Christ and with each other. John Paul II calls this the "language of the sign" or the "prophetism of the body." There were both true and false prophets in the Old Testament. That this language might be true, it must reflect all the goods

---

[163] Ibid., 434.
[164] Ibid., 506.

of marriage: fidelity (indissolubility), friendship (no manipulation), and fecundity (be open to life). This is the fullness of what marriage has to offer.

Some proponents of *Theology of the Body* have made the strange logical jump from the fact the body is good and expresses this communion of hearts to the conclusion that, by grace, man returns to a kind of Original Justice in which he need not worry about the enticements of pleasures or concupiscence of the flesh. The pope is clear that one can never return to this state and that the condemnation by the Scriptures of lust is not about the body or the passions as such but about the will. One can never act as though one can be free from temptation in this life. Though spousal love is an important part of the healing of spirit in this regard, it does not do away now with our weakness totally. "The 'hermeneutics of the sacrament' allows us to draw the conclusion that man is always *essentially 'called' and not merely 'accused,'* even inasmuch as he is precisely the 'man of concupiscence.'"[165] So, a proper understanding of the body and Marriage gives us hope but not presumption.

The pope adds his reflections on *Humanae Vitae* as a final flourish. To be true and loving, Marriage must be ethical. It must take account of both unity and life as it was indeed created by the Creator and redeemed by Christ. The pope in no sense denies the traditional natural law treatment of this matter but enriches it a thousandfold with an examination from Scripture that includes some reference to the phenomenological method but not one that denies the traditional objective doctrine. In fact, he references it often. To suggest that prolonged physical examination of the body or merely having fun in sex is what the pope has in mind is a serious misinterpretation. "If the key element of the spirituality of spouses and parents — the essential 'power' that the spouses must continually draw from their sacramental

[165] Ibid., 547.

'consecration' — is *love*, this love, as the text of the encyclical makes clear (*Humanae Vitae*, 20), is by its nature *linked with chastity, which, in turn, manifests itself as self-mastery or continence.*"[166]

John Paul II further applies his ideas in his landmark study in ethics applied to Marriage, *Love and Responsibility*. In this study, he distinguishes between use and enjoyment. This distinction between to use (*uti*) and to enjoy (*frui*), he explains, is based on the idea that, in the former, a person makes another simply a means to seek pleasure without respecting all the goods involved in the relationship. This is "to use." In the other, a person takes pleasure in something because it is good as a reflection of the perfection of a true good rooted in being. This is "to enjoy." In the latter case, the enjoyment comes from the affirmation of the good and freedom of the other.

In sexual matters, the human body should be a means of enjoyment and not of use because, reflecting the idea of the "nuptial meaning of the body" from *Theology of the Body*, it is the means by which one gives oneself as a gift to another and receives the gift of the other. For this relationship to be true and good, one must never reduce the other person to merely an object of use. In a utilitarian society, the value of the experience of pleasure is the greater good for its own sake. The good of the person becomes merely a means to pleasure. "You are good because you make me feel good."

On the other hand, in authentic enjoyment, human reason is directed to the concern of the other person for his own sake by affirming his uniqueness and freedom. Though couples may experience a legitimate pleasure in this relationship, the objective common good is the foundation of love. The pleasure is an adjunct good that often accompanies the commitment of soul of one person to the other. The sexual appetite is subjected to the common good of the relationship

---

[166] Ibid., 644.

with the other person. This true objective bond of love frees the relationship from subjectivism and egotism. Love is the unification of the persons expressing fidelity, fecundity, and friendship and not just mutually experienced pleasure. If love is looked upon as merely sensual and mutually experienced pleasure, then the person is subjected to exploitation merely to feel good.

This is the basis for the sex urge that arises in puberty and is wholly natural. This urge is not for pleasure alone, though it may be very pleasant. In fact, it is the first very powerful realization of a child of the affirmation of another person just because he is other. The child moves out of his self-centered world and experiences the world of another human being. It is oriented to the respect for the giving of life and all the relationships that turn around the natural order, which calls for a virtue between the parties rooted in the possibility of procreation. This is also the remedy for our egotistic tendencies to dominate and use another (*remedium concupiscientiae*), our portion remaining from the Original Sin. Of course, in adolescents, this is still very immature. It must be neither stifled nor engaged in with reckless abandon but controlled. A person learns both to be interested in the other sex and to control this desire in order to learn real love.

This is one of the reasons against incest or Matrimony between two relatives bound closely by blood. Human laws found impediments based on consanguinity, excluding persons too closely related by origin from contracting marriage. There is a natural shame between people living in the same family. People resist being objects of use for pleasure, and this is especially true of people with whom one has lived so closely in the early years of one's life.

St. John Paul II calls this resistance to being made a thing for pleasure the "phenomenon of shame." "Shame is a tendency, uniquely characteristic of the human person, to conceal sexual values sufficiently to prevent them from obscuring the value of the person as such."[167] This experience emerges when something that of its very nature should be private passes the bounds of privacy and becomes public. This desire to protect the freedom of his person leads one to withdraw into the interior self in order to conceal certain values from someone who is trying to manipulate the person based on those values.

Shame gives rise to sexual modesty, which is not to be identified with clothing or absence thereof. The question of the covering of the body is a secondary one to the desire of the person to preserve his spiritual integrity and freedom. The person is a potential subject for the enjoyment of another through the sexual experience, not an object just for pleasure. There is no sexual shame in children because children are not sufficiently aware of themselves as subjects to manipulate others in this way. Shame entails the desire to conceal sexual values because people might take advantage of us and reduce us to objects of use. This is the opposite of the longing to be loved for one's own sake. True self-restraining love dissolves shame.

C. S. Lewis expresses what John Paul II means by shamelessness in more general terms. When one person looks on another as merely an object for their use, " 'to be' means 'to be in competition.' "[168] A fair description of this attitude regarding sex is: "Sex might have been, from our [the demons] point of view, quite innocent. It might have been merely one more mode in which a stronger self preyed upon a weaker — as it is, indeed, among the spiders where the bride concludes her nuptials by eating her groom."[169]

Sexual intercourse between married people is not a form of legalized shamelessness or mutual manipulation. Only self-restraining love can preclude this. Shame may be experienced on many levels.

[167] John Paul II, *Love and Responsibility* (San Francisco: Ignatius Press, 1993), 187.
[168] Lewis, *The Screwtape Letters*, 81.
[169] Ibid., 81.

There is physical shame, in which a person does not present his or her body in such a way as to encourage becoming an object of pleasure. This is why we now cover our bodies with clothing. There is emotional shame, which involves the desire to conceal one's emotional and passionate reactions to others for the same reason. This is not the same as prudery, which means the concealment of one's real intentions in a personal relationship with another or about sexual matters in general. The prude pretends no interest but is really trying to dominate another sexually.

Shame cannot be judged by mere physical description. The same is true of the difference between pornography and art. Art must promote modesty, which encourages the self-restraining love in which the experience of the naked body, as in the statue of David by Michelangelo, encourages the respect and freedom for other persons. Immodesty, which also relates to pornography, is the use of the nakedness of a human body to promote an impersonal exploitation of another as an object of pleasure. The human body is something beautiful in itself, but the tendency to present it in such a way as to encourage domination and exploitation is immoral.

The conjugal act should be a means for the affirmation of the freedom, dignity, and intelligence of the other. No one should be forced into it against his will. It is possible for a man to rape his wife if he does not treat her with the dignity accorded to a human person in the relationship. St. John Paul II teaches on the text from the Sermon on the Mount concerning the lustful look: "Adultery 'committed in the heart' consists precisely in this. A man can commit such adultery 'in the heart' even with his own wife, if he treats her only as an object for the satisfaction of drives."[170] If any person is only an object of use for sexual pleasure, that person is demeaned. Love here is not just an emotional experience of a

[170] John Paul II, *Male and Female He Created Them*, 299.

storm of emotion but must be rooted in a commitment of will to affirm the individual personhood of the other. The pope teaches that for this reason, realistic sexual education of the youth is not primarily about techniques of body. It is, rather, about learning to respect the relationship of the sexual act to personal affirmation of the other and thus resist using or being used by another in a sexual relationship. It is about developing a soul characterized by self-restraining love.

The Difference between Marriage as a Natural Sacrament and Marriage in the New Testament

The difference between natural marriage and Matrimony, which is one of the seven sacraments, turns around the possibility of the spouses and the children being able to arrive at the vision of God. In the natural sacrament, the bodily and fleshly union cannot attain the vision of God because the natural sacrament as we know it exists in the condition of Original Sin. Though God created this relationship to be an image of the giving and receiving within the Trinity and the creation of life outside it, and this meaning remains after the sin, grace provides the possibility of fully realizing this meaning. After the first sin, though this is the only good left to us after the Fall, it is also characterized by concupiscence. In this concupiscence, the body retains its original value as a vehicle of giving the gift of self, but becomes an occasion where, instead of a gift for another, it is all too easy to reduce it to a means of mutual extortion. "Man, alas, is not such a perfect being that the sight of the body of another person, especially a person of the opposite sex, can arouse in him a disinterested liking which develops into an innocent affection. In practice, it also arouses concupiscence, or a wish to enjoy concentrated on sexual values with no regard to the value of the person."[171] The body, therefore, becomes a "value not sufficiently

[171] John Paul II, *Love and Responsibility*, 190.

appreciated."[172] This difficulty also introduces into the relationship the potential of use and makes it difficult for the parties to discover the original meaning of the gift marriage was created to foster. The state of original innocence ensured this gift character because of the presence of grace and the absence of sin. This right intention is compromised when the other becomes an object of use. This easily happens when all the goods of marriage are not respected. In the Old Testament, procreation was exalted at the expense of unity of the parties, and hence the practice of polygamy was adopted. In the modern world, the unitive is often exalted to the expense of the procreative, and this leads to wholesale contraception, which in turn has led to a myriad of other difficulties, not least of which in today's society is same-sex marriage. When marriage is completely divorced from childbearing, there is no real reason to condemn same-sex marriage.

Both *Humanae Vitae* and *Familiaris Consortio* affirm that every conjugal act must remain open to procreation. If this is denied by use of human devices, then the act becomes a means of mutual manipulation for power. The right intention present in marriage before the Fall, where sex was looked upon as a physical completion of the spiritual gift of self, must entail both mutual respect and the possibility of procreation should this be physically possible. On the objective level, this is found in the potential present in the act of generation. In marriage before the Fall and marriage as it now exists in light of redemption from the Fall, the children have the potential to arrive at the final good, which is the Beatific Vision, through grace.

After the Fall, because of a lack of grace, man was unable to attain the supernatural order, and so marriage became a sign oriented to recovering this gift, which could only be done through redemption. It was thus a natural sacrament in which both the qualities of unity

[172] John Paul II, *Male and Female He Created Them*, 307.

and procreation were present, but neither the parties nor the children could attain the Beatific Vision by the practice of marriage alone. It remained as a sign oriented to disinterested love, but without grace, this was almost impossible to realize. Of course, there were people under grace in the dispensation of the Old Law, but this was based on their desire for redemption, which involved an implicit faith, albeit for many centuries very obscure, in Christ. Once grace is attained in the redemption, the child and the relationship can arrive again at the fullness of their original meaning in creation, which was to love God and to strive to live with Him forever.

One can see a prelude to this in the marriage of Joachim and Ann and their attendant participation in the conception of the Blessed Virgin. Christian Marriage adds the dimension of being a sign of the redemptive love of the high priest, Christ. It is a sacrament connected to His sacrifice, and so each spouse is a priest to the other. It is the primary example of the priesthood of the laity in which each baptized person participates in helping the other to die to self and live to disinterested love.

The difference between pagan marriage and Christian Marriage is found primarily in the fact that, because of the redemption, both the parties and the children can again attain the true end of providence, union with the one God, and that the spouses die to utilitarian considerations to live again the meaning of complete self-giving. Natural marriage, though good, could only be a means to living acquired virtue and a disposition to a future redemption.

The final purpose of sacramental Marriage according to St. Thomas is to prepare the children for the *cultus Dei* (the worship of God). He is speaking here not only of the worship of the seven sacraments in this life but also of the definitive worship of God that occurs in Heaven without sacraments. For all these reasons, Marriage in Christ must be accompanied by a special blessing of the Church through the priest.

It is true that the baptized couple are the ministers of Marriage. But this ministry is not carried out in private and so must be connected to the public witness and worship of the Church. The priest or deacon witnesses the Marriage in the name of the Church because of the new moral dimension obtained from the prefect completion now rendered possible by Christ of the forces present in creation. Non-Catholic Christians often recognize other forms for this same reality, but Catholics are bound to this form.

Sinful man, through the natural sacrament of Marriage, is rooted in perpetual existence through children. Marriage in the New Testament completes this mystery through resurrection. By the conception of children, the species in general exists perpetually. By the resurrection, each individual exists immortally. To perpetuate the redemption and the final fulfillment of each person in this, the sacrament of Matrimony was instituted by Christ. No one can people Heaven or rise from the dead if there are no people. The duty to become fruitful and multiply has a new dimension. Christ recovers the original meaning of marriage as an image of the Trinity and the creation and adds the further dimension of redemptive love in the Spirit. A new perfecting quality is introduced into the relationship. Now, one suffers to rid oneself of concupiscence precisely to recover disinterested love after the manner of the Creator.

The original goods of fidelity, friendship, and fecundity are not changed in the sacrament of the New Testament, but they receive a further moral quality. This quality is a preparation for Heaven despite our tendencies to egotism and domination. The character of the consent also takes on a new perfection of nature by redeeming grace.

Marriage fulfills nature. But a distinction must be made about nature. Something may be said to be natural when it is necessary. This is not what is meant by the fulfillment of nature in marriage. Something may also be natural by way of an inclination in nature that must be morally completed by the freedom born of the intellect and will. Though man shares the natural good of generation with animals because his genus is that of animal, these must be realized in freedom and choice because he is a rational animal. This is not an absolute freedom. He cannot change the goods by his will. It is a participated or proprietary freedom according to which he embraces these goods morally.

This is true both of the procreation, which is oriented to the final purpose of union with God Himself in Heaven, and the unity of the parties who participate in their act of love in realizing the image of God in man by a disinterested interpersonal giving of themselves to each other. The generative act in man and the relationship whose loving union is directly based on it differs from that of animals, first, in the object which is its fruit, the body ensouled by a spirit, and, second, in the kind of mutual personal relationship enjoyed by those who participate in it, one of disinterested love and not of use for pleasure. Of course, the parties take a legitimate pleasure in such an action. This is that of a reasoned good enjoyed, not used simply for the sake of pleasure.

John Paul II expresses it well: "Christian marriage and the Christian family build up the Church: for in the family the human person is not only brought into being and progressively introduced by means of education into the human community, but by means of the rebirth of baptism and education in the faith, the child is introduced into God's family, which is the Church."[173]

Thus, Marriage in the New Law of Christ takes on a different dimension. The children (*proles*) can arrive at the vision of God and not just have a passive capacity for it; the relationship between man and wife (*fides*) and the bond (*sacramentum*) become a sign of the love of Christ for His Church that led Him to become obedient unto death and die on the Cross.

---

[173] John Paul II, *Familiaris Consortio*, no. 15.

Before and after the first sin and in redemption, marriage has a variety of theological meanings, all of which are related to each other. Before sin, marriage was ordered to the good of children and the parties in imitation of the inner life of the Trinity and the manner in which God brings forth and supports life toward the common destiny of the universe in creation. After sin, it becomes a remedy for the wound of sin (*remedium concupiscientiae*) determined by the law of nature and persons in the Law of Moses and an image of the redemptive love wrought by Christ on the Cross and implemented by the sacraments. Since marriage is also of great use for the development of physical and spiritual life in the home, it is also subject of civil law, friendship and mutual service, inheritance, and the like. The relationship before the first sin makes marriage an office of nature; the second shows how Marriage is a sacrament, and the third, an institution of the civil order.

Contraception versus Natural Family Planning

The Church, then, emphasizes procreation heavily but not exclusively as one of the essential elements of marriage. To be sure, this does not mean that one needs to intend to have a child in every single marital act. This also does not mean that one must have as many children as possible. One may limit birth, but this is not the same as contraception or birth control. To understand the difference between the recommendation of the Church for self-control of the parties based on the natural infertility in the woman's cycle and contraception, one must again refer to the distinction made by St. John Paul II between using and enjoying. These are not two methods of contraception, one of which is simply permitted by authority and the other rejected. They emphasize two completely different moral objects and so are based on two essentially different worldviews. "Thus, the fundamental task of the family is to serve life, to actualize in history the original blessing of the Creator — that of transmitting by procreation the divine image from person to person."[174]

Contraception is based on a worldview that separates children from the act of marriage. It is one of the reasons why same-sex marriage is finally triumphing in the Western world. This is an attack on traditional marriage such as it has been known in Judeo-Christian culture for thousands of years. It also leads to an inhuman lack of moral restraint and formation for members of society and promotes making people objects of use for pleasure. As soon as a human being becomes a liability for the selfish use of the individual, they may be sacrificed, even killed. Thus, contraception destroys a self-restraining morality, honor, and even moral freedom. In making people objects of use for subjective need, it also paves the way for the culture of death in abortion and euthanasia.

France was one of the first countries to undercut objective morality in marriage and encourage contraception. Dr. Baars reflects on the fruit of this mentality in his experience of Buchenwald, in which people were systematically killed just to get more food.

> Once on the battlefields of World War I, now in the concentration camps of World War II, France paid the price for taking the lead in one of the most successful campaigns in modern history some one hundred and twenty five years earlier: the campaign of birth control. Successful their campaign has been, because birth control appeals so much to the selfish element in every human being. It eliminates the responsibilities and duties of love, it decries the consequence of romance, and it educates young people in their own selfish interest and

[174] Ibid., no. 28.

in the indulgence of their selfish pleasures. France, by destroying the morality of its youth, had led the way to the destruction of its own existence; it had removed from its children the backbone of perseverance against evil.[175]

St. John Paul II again explains this well. It is worth quoting at length.

In the light of the experience of many couples and of the data provided by the different human sciences, theological reflection is able to perceive and is called to study further the difference, both anthropological and moral, between contraception and recourse to the rhythm of the cycle; it is a difference which is much wider and deeper than is usually thought, one which involves in the final analysis two irreconcilable concepts of the human person and human sexuality. The choice of the natural rhythms involves accepting the cycle of the person, that is, the woman, and thereby accepting dialogue, reciprocal respect, shared responsibility and self-control. To accept the cycle and to enter into dialogue means to recognize both the spiritual and corporeal character of conjugal communion, and to live personal love with its requirement of fidelity. In this context, the couple comes to experience how conjugal communion is enriched with those values of tenderness and affection which constitute the inner soul of human sexuality in its physical dimension also. In this way sexuality is respected and promoted in its truly and fully human dimension, and is never "used" as an "object" that, by breaking

[175] Conrad Baars, *Doctor of the Heart* (Alba House: New York, 1996), 110.

the personal unity of soul and body, strikes at God's creation itself at the level of the deepest interaction between nature and person.[176]

The difference between natural family planning and contraception can be delineated in six points:

- Natural family planning (NFP) is an example of enjoyment and, so, is person-oriented. Contraception is an example of making another an object of use and, so, is pleasure-oriented.

- NFP affirms both the subject and the object because it respects objective morals and does so as a free exercise of virtue. Contraception affirms only the subject and denies the objective order.

- NFP is not a method of birth control and, so, is not utilitarian. Contraception is simply a method.

- NFP respects divine providence because God Himself has placed the natural infertility in the woman's cycle. Still, the act remains open to God's action should He will to give a child. Contraception seeks to deny the role of providence in childbearing and, hence, God's governance of sexuality. It is a technique created by man against the creative potential in human fertility.

- NFP is morally good if it flows also from a right intention that affirms personal love. This depends on the intellect and will and is an example

[176] John Paul II, *Familiaris Consortio*, no. 32.

of choice for chastity. It also involves self-control. It is a virtue. Contraception is simply against conception.

- NFP unites the natural and personal order and encourages communication among the parties. Contraception separates the natural and personal orders. No real personal communication or interest is necessary provided both the parties get pleasure out of it.

The practice of NFP must be based on the good of the other person and cannot be done for a trivial motive or when circumstances do not warrant it. All things being equal, marriage is oriented to family and, so, to children. It would be wrong to postpone having children indefinitely or to limit oneself to one or two. This requires one to respect the order of nature and the possibility of parenthood found in the act. The moral aspect of NFP demands that it be done from love for the other and as an act of the virtue of chastity. It is not just another method of birth control. Continence and chastity are not ends in themselves but are rooted in the affirmation of the person of the other, which in turn is based on the presence of the spiritual soul. Because the person is a spirit, no person may be reduced to an object of use, but every person must be a subject of love.

In the practice of chastity in the sexual relationship, man rediscovers the original innocence in which the body was a means to express the gift of love in the soul. To submit this experience to the order of providence is to respect the hierarchy of values wherein lower things find their perfection in higher and deeper things; matter finds its perfection in spirit. This is because reason permeates the otherwise biological actions of man.

Chastity for the Kingdom of God

One psychiatrist said of the modern seminary that it often turns men into boys. Many people decry virginity and celibacy because they think that this is a deviant and unnatural life. One priest in the late 60s lamented as he left the priesthood to marry that without a woman, he was only half a man.

This problem will always be with the Church as long as contemporary culture regards virginity and celibacy as simply a negative state in which people renounce marriage without examining it any more deeply. In fact, though it is true that virginity and celibacy are exceptional for the manner in which spousal love is lived in this world, they in no sense involve a rejection of the spousal love by which a person gives himself exclusively to another. In fact, they realize the same potential in man but in a supernatural way. They are not a rejection of spousal love but an embracing of it on a deeper and completely supernatural level. Their exceptional state is due to the fact they give this love in a manner appropriate to Christ and Heaven and depend on an individual grace. "Whoever denigrates marriage also diminishes the glory of virginity. Whoever praises it makes virginity more admirable and resplendent. What appears good in comparison with evil would not be truly good. The most excellent good is something even better than what is admitted to be good."[177]

To be celibate means to be mature enough in one's emotional and spiritual life to be alone without being lonely. The person mature enough to be celibate is the person mature enough to commit himself freely in response to the grace given him by God to either the married or celibate and virginal state because he is a free and self-possessed individual blessed with the grace of baptism. The celibate person has

---

[177] John Chrysostom, *De Virginitate* 10:1: PG 48, 540, quoted in *CCC* 1620 and reflecting John Paul II, *Familiaris Consortio*, no. 16.

come to love himself selflessly, so much so that his love is the same love of the saints and angels in Heaven, where "they neither marry nor are given in marriage" (Matt. 22:30). It will be remembered that the Lord spoke these words in response to the question of divorce and indissolubility of Marriage. This is not due to a utilitarian perspective based on some denigration of Marriage. It demands the attitude of Christ from the Cross, who sees the world from a supernatural aspect and loves all while dying for them.

Because of a special grace, the celibate person is free to be a man without giving himself exclusively to one person only. Instead, by giving himself completely to God, he offers his life for every person. He can be love without having to "make love." Those in marriage who practice marital chastity by periodic continence do so by a joyful restraint fed by the personal affirmation of the other. In the religious or priestly state, this is due to a special consecration in which the freedom of restraint allows them to personally affirm the whole human race and have millions of spiritual children without using genital sexuality.

This is rooted in a special way according to the personalistic norm already cited of *Gaudium et Spes* and John Paul II: No person may be an object of use, but every person must be a subject of love, and a person only realizes his nature by a sincere disinterested gift of himself to another. This, in turn, affirms not just the rights of the love of the Creator for His creation. When one accepts this objective moral order, one participates in the order of the Creator, Whose rights over creation are all-encompassing. One gives the nuptial betrothed love of his person to God as a person exclusively and attains the unique fulfillment of all that it means to be one subject to God's plan. He also witnesses to a unique realization of God's providence by not limiting his experience of love to one or to a few people but giving the gift of himself to the entire human race. The human soul that is espoused to God gives self to God alone. Mystical virginity essentially pledges conjugal love to God as an object of the will in love. Priestly love essentially pledges all that the priest is to Christ and His Church so that when he offers the sacrifice for the living and the dead with Christ the High Priest and says, "This is my body," it is true in every sense of the word. He is acting not in his own person in the Mass but *in persona Christi capitis* (in the person of Christ the High Priest), the true priest and victim in every celebration of the sacrifice of the Mass, which is eternal. As long as physical continence is present in both states, the possibility of such a mystery and pledge remains.

Betrothed or spousal love in Marriage has a terrestrial and temporal dimension of personal affirmation. The celibate and the virgin practice spiritual affirmation of all men from the perspective of eternal life. The image of a God who gives all is seen in Marriage and receives a special application in celibacy and virginity. This is not due to the superiority of the spiritual over the material, because both married people and those who practice virginity are called to do so from grace. The value is based on the role virginity and celibacy play in realizing Heaven on earth. The one, virginity as a fixed way of life; the other, celibacy, as an image of Christ the priest through Whom alone such life can be obtained. The source of the teaching of the Church that virginity is a higher state is based on the primacy of Heaven itself as the ultimate end and contemplation as a participation in that state. "The evangelical counsels, by which Christ invites some people to share his experience as the chaste, poor and obedient one, call for and make manifest in those who accept them an explicit desire to be totally conformed to Christ.... This is why the Christian tradition has always spoken of the objective superiority of the consecrated life."[178]

---

[178] John Paul II, apostolic exhortation *Vita Consecrata* (March 25, 1996), no. 18.

The sign value of virginity comes from the fact that it manifests life returned in the final sense to the Creator as final cause. The virginal person anticipates the future resurrection and so is an "eschatological sign." It is also a recollection of life before the first sin and so provides a powerful stimulus to married and single people struggling with concupiscence of the true freedom of grace. This must all be guaranteed by the fact that it is caused by grace and rooted in the gift of self completely to God in response to being loved by Him. Thus, the moral will of the gift is its essence as a state that presumes physical virginity but is not exclusively defined by it. Spiritual fatherhood and motherhood are embraced by married people for their family. They are also embraced by the priest and religious but for the whole human race. As physical fatherhood and motherhood find their completion in spiritual parenting, so with the virgin or the celibate, spiritual fatherhood and motherhood are of its essence without physical parenting. For the priest, this includes being a strong male role model capable of tenderness but also courageous in struggling for his diocese or parish. In the case of consecrated persons, this involves also empathy for the whole human race realized in prayer, sacrifice, and the good works of the community and specific institute.

NINE

Family and Education

The family has four dimensions that grow out of the relationship of Marriage, all of which must be protected and promoted by the greater society and the Church. These are essential to both the principle of organic growth in society and subsidiarity.

The first is that the family is natural and thus cannot be interfered with or replaced by the State. The family is not made by the common consent of human beings and so is not the result of positive law. It is, rather, closely connected to the act of childbearing, which is one of the two essential purposes of the marriage act and so is established by God. It is a real virtual unity of will founded on the personal participation of the husband and wife in the order of providence. This is realized in both the procreation *and* the education of the children. The family must, therefore, involve moral participation that is free and virtuous. The participation of each on their own level, of both parents of opposite sexes and the children, is thus essential to the realizing of the good and happiness of the members of this most basic of human communities. The protection of the family by positive right is also of a juridical nature. Civil society cannot dissolve the family or seek to replace it without causing chaos in the civil order. The family is also of an economic nature. Since a decent standard of living and social peace are necessary to provide the correct environment for the family to be formed in a disinterested way, the Church has always maintained that the morality and progress of the economy must be primarily related to the society of the family and not the State. The principle good of the economic order is the satisfaction of the daily spiritual and physical needs necessary for the promotion of the family.

Because the family is rooted in divine providence turning around the sexual act, the order of authority is rooted in the personal participation of the father and the mother in the act of procreation. The parents supply the matter, but God directly creates the form of the human soul. The diverse participation of the parents in the act determines the order of authority and responsibility in which each participates in authority.

As is true of every human community, authority is primarily an application of the virtue of prudence. This prudence is different than the prudence connected to the authority of a civil or ecclesiastical community because it represents the unique good pursued in the family. That primary good is education. This education is primarily interested in inculcating virtues, whether natural or Christian, in all the members of the household. "The fecundity of conjugal love cannot be reduced solely to the procreation of children, but must extend to their moral education and spiritual formation. 'The role of parents in education is of such importance that it is almost impossible to provide an adequate substitute.' The right and duty of parents to education their children are primordial and inalienable.... The home is well-suited for education in the virtues" (CCC 2221, 2223).

Homer's epic poem, The Odyssey, tells the tale of a broken home. The Greek king Ulysses has gone away to fight the Trojan War. At the end of the war, he is forced by the gods to wander for ten years before he can return home. During that time, his home is filled with chaos. The public room of the house is occupied by suitors for the hand of his wife, Penelope, who cleverly eludes their suits. Still, her cleverness is not enough to keep chaos from the house. Without the presence of the man to protect the family, the suitors fill the house with one continuous din. The one who suffers most from this chaos is Ulysses's son, Telemachus, who, as with modern youth, is completely uneasy about his identity when he does not experience his father's spiritual care. Homer shows an astonishing knowledge of human nature, for the youth only rediscovers his identity when his father returns to reassert his spiritual presence by taking possession of the household, purging it of chaos, and revealing his identity to his son and his wife. One could say only when both parents are spiritually and emotionally present to the child can the child really discover his unique identity as a person.

The *Catechism of the Catholic Church* echoes Homer's insight, which is also expressed by Catholic teaching, when it quotes Vatican II, "By its very nature the institution of marriage and married love is ordered to the procreation and education of offspring and it is in them that it finds its crowning glory" (CCC 1652). While the procreative dimension has been a subject of lively literature spawned by the birth control debate in recent years in the Church, the educative dimension has been the subject of less lively interest. Yet it is just as important, if for no other reason than the secular assault that occurs constantly in most public and many parochial schools now on the Catholic values of the students. This is also because education of spirit is the natural complement of procreation in the flesh. In spiritual parenting, Christian parenting, father and mother become domestic priests. They complete their cooperation with God in physical birth by cooperating in the child's spiritual birth.

The relationship of Marriage is perfected in the nurturing of life. Because human life is spiritual, the nurture of life includes the spiritual nurturing of the seed of divine life to which the soul is called. This calling to divine life is so central to the perfection of man that Thomas Aquinas says there is "something divine" about the human seed. This is because human seed sown through the act of procreation must end in the spiritual soul. As the soul is the life of the body, so God is the life of the soul. Little trinities come forth by procreation. Since man comes forth from God in His divine image, man can only be complete when this divine image is complete. Little trinities can only fully become themselves in union with *the Trinity*. This happens when grace is completed in the vision of God in Heaven. St. Thomas goes so far as to maintain that it is the life-long nurturing of the spiritual life that prepares for the vision of God in the souls of children, which is the natural foundation of the indissolubility of Marriage.

Education of soul, then, is a more essential mission of the family than nourishment of the body. Parents have a necessary and inalienable right to nourish the minds of their children by spiritual instruction because this alone completes their physical procreation. Pope John Paul II has expressed this very well: "The right and duty of parents to give education is *essential*, since it is connected with the transmission of human life; it is *original and primary* with regard to the educational role of others, on account of the uniqueness of the loving relationship between parents and children; and it is *irreplaceable and inalienable,* and therefore incapable of being entirely delegated to others or usurped by others."[179]

This natural duty and right of education is true of every family by nature. In the Christian family, in which all the members are blessed by a sacrament of grace, it takes on a new and wonderful dimension. The Christian family nourishes the whole life of grace, which includes reason, prayer, moral life, and theological faith. This is the reason why

[179]John Paul II, apostolic exhortation *Familiaris Consortio* (November 22, 1981), no. 36.

the Church has always called the family the *ecclesia domestica*, the domestic church. Christian parents nurture the Word in their children by conforming themselves to Christ. The basis of this conformity is the "character," or indelible mark, which they received in Baptism. This character of conformity to Christ is so intrinsic to the parents that their lives are a constant offering made to God that finds its power in the worship the Christ Himself in His soul offers continuously to His Father in Heaven. One beautiful application of this character is the sacrament of Matrimony. By virtue of the character of Baptism, Christian Marriage is an act of worship in which the spouses are the ministers, or priests, to one another. This is the principal sacrament in which the priesthood of the laity is found.

Another beautiful application of this character of conformity to Christ is the participation of Christian parents in the education of the souls of their children. In this, they exercise their role as prophets who teach the truth and fulfill their share in the common priesthood of Christ. "So great and splendid is the educational ministry of Christian parents that St. Thomas [Aquinas] has no hesitation in comparing it with the ministry of priest."[180] They live, teach, and guide as domestic priests because the children grow in holiness through their influence. They are true other Christs to their children and prepare them in their self-offering on earth for the worship of God in Heaven. Physical and spiritual paternity and maternity reach their summit in spiritual paternity, especially in instruction in taking the sacraments. "Human beings will come particularly close to God when the *spiritual parenthood of which God is the prototype* takes shape in them."[181]

Though the Catholic school can be a powerful extension of the right and duty of the parents to grow in holiness by educating their children,

---

[180] Ibid., no. 38.
[181] Ibid., no. 36.

when a number of Catholic schools are teaching secular humanism, homeschooling is certainly a fitting expression of the parents as priest, prophet, and king. In fact, this is the central apostolate of Marriage. The parents are the apostles of the children.

However, though homeschooling can be a fitting option to ensure Catholic teaching, those who choose it must ensure that the child learns appropriate socializing skills and does not become isolated. A well-rounded education would also take care that the appropriate education of the heart in things like friendships, service to others, resolving discord, courtesy, and education in social situations is not lacking. Education must involve the whole person.

In exercising their apostolate, parents should be sure that their education is based on a correct understanding of the nature of man. Modern education has many faults based on the error that the satisfaction of the passions is the *exclusive* purpose of education. Philosophies such as that of Rousseau dominate the scene. He believed that reason was the enemy of the soul to such an extent that the man who contemplates was a depraved animal to him. The purpose of the teacher is not to impart knowledge but merely to provide a milieu in which the child can express the divine in himself. There is no discipline or interest in self-control. This philosophy of education places an exaggerated faith in the unfettered freedom of the human person to set his own limits and find his own truth. It is incompatible with Catholicism and also sound philosophy because it fails to find any truth outside the subject.

An equally difficult philosophy of education is the Lowood School of the *Jane Eyre* tradition. This looks upon human nature in children as naturally the enemy of grace. According to this school, grace must destroy a nature that is totally depraved. Just because education entails to some extent the control of the passions, one must not, therefore, conclude that education involves the complete destruction of the passions and the senses by reason.

Real Catholic ideals support the very evident truth that everyone's soul is naturally ordered to God. The fact that we experience a difficulty in realizing this order due to Original Sin means that our nature is wounded, not that nature is evil in itself. Spiritual parenthood should, therefore, take advantage of the natural tendency to order in the child, while realizing that the child needs guidance according to his age to slowly act in conformity with this tendency.

Just as ministerial priests must adapt their message to the capabilities of the congregation, so the parents, as the lay priests, must adapt theirs to the age and experience of the child. While not swerving one iota from the basic truths of Catholicism, they must present them in a manner and at a time when the young minds they are forming can best absorb them. This takes the humility of an apostle.

The mission to educate, then, is a direct result of the power of procreation. It involves the perfection of an act that was begun in procreation and must be completed in the perfection of both the human body and the soul. Education is found primarily in the parent, and it is the right and duty of the parent to care for it. Their mission in this cannot be completely delegated to another, especially to the State.

Though the family is the principle agent of education, it does not therefore follow that it is the exclusive agent of education. Both civil and religious authorities share a responsibility with the parents, but as an extension of the primary education given by the family. The family is not the only community necessary for human development. "Family ties are not absolute" (CCC 2232). The Church, the State, and the family all have complementary roles in the perfection of man and the human soul. Subsidiarity demands that each educate according to the measure their community contributes to the perfection of the soul. The family is the first school of those moral virtues necessary for social living and, with respect to religion, is a domestic church when young people first learn their faith, about God and their relationship to Him.

In learning disinterested self-love on this level, they prepare the bedrock for the further development of this love in civil and infused virtue.

Thus, both the Church and the State have certain rights because the child is a citizen of each. The State has the right and duty to ensure that education will equip the child to play his proper role as a good and productive citizen in the civil order. The Church has a right to demand that the catechesis of children be sufficient before they admit them to further sacraments after Baptism.

The State also can protect the right of the child when parenting is found lacking or even destructive. The Church has the right to be sure the child can develop religiously through the sacraments and preaching of the Church. To forbid the Church to sponsor and promote educational institutions in which Christian children are educated in their Faith is clearly immoral and an unjust usurpation on the part of civil power.

The Christian father and mother share in the mission of educating their children on three levels. First, as the principal teachers of good and virtue to the children, they clarify the truth and so have a true prophetic mission. They also encourage the children to practice the truth in love.

The order of grace refers to those actions by which man receives grace, the sacraments. So the father and mother encourage and implement the sacramental life in their children. When one understands and receives the love of grace, this stimulates one to love in grace also. The interior disposition of divine love leads to a kind of integrity that makes one a servant of others, just as Christ laid down His life for others. Since the person who can serve others well must be gifted with prudence in a special way, that person is also a monarch. He can rule himself and rule by serving the good in others. The kingly role of Christ is an offering of self for the good of others. These two levels in turn reflect dispositive grace, by which man is strengthened in conversion, and executive grace, by which he lives out the consecration of Baptism.

The prophetic role perfects the intellect, the priestly perfects the will, and the kingly role places these both at the service of society, whether in the family itself, in the State, or in the Church.

In response to the Fascist attempt to unify all education exclusively in the State to the denial of the parents, Pius XI was very clear about these various levels and responsibilities. His teaching is worth quoting at length here:

> Education is essentially a social and not a mere individual activity. Now there are three necessary societies, distinct from one another and yet harmoniously combined by God, into which man is born: two, namely the family and civil society, belong to the natural order; the third, the Church, to the supernatural order.
>
> And first of all education belongs preeminently to the Church, by reason of a double title in the supernatural order, conferred exclusively upon her by God Himself; absolutely superior therefore to any other title in the natural order.
>
> The first title is founded upon the express mission and supreme authority to teach, given her by her divine Founder.... The second title is the supernatural motherhood, in virtue of which the Church, spotless spouse of Christ, generates, nurtures and educates souls in the divine life of grace, with her Sacraments and her doctrine.
>
> The family therefore holds directly from the Creator the mission and hence the right to educate the offspring, a right inalienable because inseparably joined to the strict obligation, a right anterior to any right whatever of civil society and of the State, and therefore inviolable on the part of any power on earth.

Now this end and object, the common welfare in the temporal order, consists in that peace and security in which families and individual citizens have the free exercise of their rights, and at the same time enjoy the greatest spiritual and temporal prosperity possible in this life, by the mutual union and co-ordination of the work of all. The function therefore of the civil authority residing in the State is twofold, to protect and to foster, but by no means to absorb the family and the individual, or to substitute itself for them.[182]

[182] Pius XI, encyclical letter *Divini Illius Magistri* (December 31, 1929), nos. 11, 15, 16, 17, 32, 43. The same doctrine is taught in *Familiaris Consortio*.

TEN
The Theology of Work

The question of the theology of work is central to a broad, practical solution to what has been called the "social question" since the Industrial Revolution in the early nineteenth century. Thus, popes have always maintained that the issue of the just wage for work is the key to the solution of this question. "The key problem of social ethics in this case is the just remuneration for work done."[183] Since the difficulty is rooted in the Industrial Revolution as a part of the theological analysis of the problem, it is necessary to examine the history of this question to appreciate the developments that have occurred in social teaching since the nineteenth century.

The most important point is that the economic order is related to and sustains the domestic order. Even without the political order, there still must be an order in which a man obtains his daily bread and the family is supported. The necessity of work and material goods would have applied even in Eden. St. John Paul II defines work as "any

---

[183] John Paul II, encyclical letter *Laborem Exercens* (September 14, 1981), no. 19.

activity by man, whether manual or intellectual, whatever its nature or circumstances."[184] Man is called to work. It is one of the characteristics of his nature that sets him apart from the animals. The capacity for work, which is therefore a characteristic of the human spirit, is also directly related to the question of those material goods necessary for the maintenance of family life. This, in contemporary terms, gives rise to the question of labor, capital, and private property. The Church's teaching on this is complex and organically develops from the issue of the connection and necessity of material goods for the progress of man.

The initial context for this is supplied in Genesis 1:28 when God commands man, after his creation in the image and likeness of God: "Be fruitful and multiply, and fill the earth and subdue it." This domination on the part of man over nature is based on the superiority of the spirit over matter and also the fact that human beings are not angels. Since man has a body, material goods are necessary for his life, as well as his happiness. This original dominion (*dominio*) is not absolute. Though man is a spirit, he did not create matter but is placed in lordship over it as a steward. "In the beginning God entrusted the earth and its resources to the common stewardship of mankind to take care of them, master them by labor, and enjoy their fruits" (CCC 2402). Man thus participates with and at the direction of God in his dominion over material goods in light of their proper use and not as though creating their substance.

In Eden, this dominion would entail the right and duty to work. This work would not have been toilsome though. Since man was filled with grace and respect for God's dominion, he would also not have exploited the earth or others for selfish and egotistical purposes. He would exercise this dominion by the power to procure and dispense material goods through possession (*possessio*). This possession would have been expressed in each being given according to his need and

---

[184] Ibid., introduction.

contribution. Material goods would have been placed under the common use of the whole human race, as indeed it still is in religious communities. Again, the reason this worked was because man before the sin was in the state of grace, and perhaps a continued state of infused contemplation, and there was no sin or unbridled egotism. He did not seek to say "Mine" of anything. In *The Screwtape Letters*, C. S. Lewis expresses the exact opposite of this attitude by having Satan say:

> And all the time the joke is that the word "mine" in its fully possessive sense cannot be uttered by a human being about anything. In the long run either Our Father or the Enemy will say "mine" of each thing that exists, and especially of each man. They will find out in the end, never fear, to whom their time, their souls, and their bodies really belong — certainly not to *them*, whatever happens. At present the Enemy says "mine" of everything on the pedantic, legalistic ground that He made it. Our Father hopes in the end to say "mine" of all things on the more realistic and dynamic ground of conquest.[185]

This possession is the origin of the famous "universal destination" of human goods, which is necessary for determining the reality of theft. In emergency situations, such as droughts or famines, the universal destination of human goods takes precedence over private property, which did not exist in Eden because it was not necessary. "The goods of creation are destined for the whole human race.... The universal destination of goods remains primordial, even if the promotion of the common good requires respect for the right to private property and its exercise" (CCC 2402–3).

[185] C. S. Lewis, *The Screwtape Letters* (New York: Macmillan Publishing Company, 1961), 98–99.

With the sin, all this changes. Without grace, the human race cannot arrive at union with God, which alone can satisfy the human soul. Other things are substituted for God that cannot possibly give the same satisfaction. Human beings try to control those things that they perceive can bring them happiness, perfection, and satisfaction. One of these is material goods.

Two weaknesses follow from this. The first is that competition enters economics. This is not a healthy competition to provide a better good or service but is solely motivated by the desire to increase wealth at the expense of another. The second is that man now thinks he is the absolute master of the material world and can do what he likes with it. It is there to be exploited, not used and enjoyed. The earth itself resists this disordered exploitation, which is rooted in the disordered human ego. Work now becomes toilsome because the earth itself resists being used. "Cursed is the earth in your work: with labor and toil shall you eat thereof all the days of your life. Thorns and thistles shall it bring forth to you, and you shall eat the herbs of the earth. In the sweat of your face shall you eat bread and return to the earth out of which you were taken" (Gen. 3:17–19).

In the light of Original Sin, the institution of private property (*proprietas*) enters this situation as the best way to ensure each person will have what he needs as a conclusion of the more general rights of the natural law of procuring and dispensing goods. It is a conclusion of human reason concerning the best way to defend the human right to both work and enjoy the fruits of one's labor in support of the family. It is, therefore, a natural right but falls under the *ius gentium*, or Right of Nations. Capital is a reflection of this right to private property, but as a conclusion of human reason, which in turn is based on the stewardship of man over nature. It does not obey intrinsic laws of inevitable historical development. Instead, capital and private property are rooted in the personal and rational order. Property is a demonstrative conclusion from the principles of the natural law, which encourage man to develop his material goods for his own personal perfection and for the perfection of the common good of society.

There is, thus, a twofold competence in material things: The power of procuring and dispensing goods, which is the source of the ability of man to possess things that are his own, and the power of common usage of good. No man is entitled to manage goods merely for himself, but he must do so in the interests of the common good and thus share them with others. There is a common right to participation in goods. This does not mean common property. The distribution of property itself is determined by positive right. Property is a natural right but not an absolute right. It was born in the Original Sin as a protection for possession of goods.

The actual method of fixing how property will be determined and the practical means to implementing it in any given society are a matter of positive law based on natural law. The final and formal cause for the existence of property is the service one expects from it. This would be realized morally in providing a just good or service and the payment of a just wage. Private ownership is subordinated morally to the common use, and practices such as occult compensation and state use of private goods in public emergencies are not justified theft. Rather, they are a recognition that with the right to property is the corresponding duty to develop it for the common good. "The right of private property, acquired or received in a just way, does not do away with the original gift of the earth to the whole of mankind.... There is no theft if consent can be presumed or if refusal is contrary to the reason and the universal destination of goods. This is the case in obvious and urgent necessity when the only way to provide for immediate essential needs (food, shelter, clothing...) is to put at one's disposal and use the property of others" (CCC 2403, 2408).

In some societies, property is not necessary to guarantee that each will be given according to his need. Such is the case with religious communities, where property is normally held in common. Often, however, because of the possessiveness and desire to dominate that the human race inherits from Adam, community of possession of goods is an occasion of discord.

In the nineteenth century, this whole picture underwent a lamentable revision. This gave rise to the social question that was first addressed by the Church in the encyclical *Rerum Novarum* written by Leo XIII in 1891. Most of the major encyclicals have subsequently been written for anniversaries of this original one: *Quadragesimo Anno* (1931), *Laborem Exercens* (1981), and *Centesimus Annus* (1991). Work is a constant factor in all questions of social peace. The essential qualities of human work are the basic key to solving these difficulties.

Objective and Subjective Work

Man is called to work in creation and dominate the earth. The problem of human work has now become a world question. This occupies a central expression of man's existence as a spirit in a body because it shows his application of reason to matter. Both faith and reason teach that work is a transitive action because it begins in the human subject and is directed to the perfection of an external object or situation. This, together with the giving and perfecting of life, fulfills the original order of creation.

Work has a twofold meaning. Objectively, it denotes the means of production of technology by which man's dominion over the earth is perfected. The original industrialization in the Industrial Revolution gave rise to the exact place of the worker regarding these means. Man is the proper subject of work. Indeed, the machine does not represent his capacity for work. This has its origin in his reason and the fact that he is a spirit. The machine is simply the means by which he carries out this dominion in an easier way. The machine is, therefore, only a tool. The ethical challenge of the Industrial Revolution is to resolve the tension created by the worker and technology in such a way that the worker is not viewed as simply a more sophisticated machine and remunerated as such.

Work also has a subjective sense. This refers to the person who performs the work. "Man has to subdue the earth and dominate it because as an 'image of God' he is a person, a subjective being capable of acting in a planned and rational way, capable of deciding about himself, and with a tendency to self-realization."[186] In work, man confirms and realizes the primacy of reason over the whole material world.

Since his work is primarily a postulate of his rationality, human work has an ethical value of its own that must be respected. This led Aristotle to distinguish between art (*techne*) and the person who works (*ethike*) in his explanation of human virtue. Art perfects something outside the person and so is judged by the work done. Ethics perfects the soul and is judged not so much by the product as by the interior formation of the producer. Art makes the work good; ethics makes both the work and the worker good. As a result, what might be technologically perfect might be ethically destructive. A surgeon may perform a brilliant surgery but, if its purpose is forced sterilization, it makes him a wicked man. The primary purpose of work is for man, not man for work. The purpose of developing economics must always have a human dimension.

In materialist thought, such as that which has characterized the Western world since the Enlightenment, work is a commodity to be bought and sold according to one deterministic law, supply and demand for profit. There is certainly nothing wrong with seeking the maximum profit through the marketplace provided that this is not the end but the means to ensure human development. Seeking profit alone through mechanistic means is very dangerous for society because it treats work as an impersonal force completely divorced from the person who does it. Man might easily be reduced to just another tool for the production of matter. This is the danger in the approach of liberal capitalism. The only value of work is the growth of business itself with no other

---

[186] John Paul II, *Laborem Exercens*, no. 6.

value needed to adapt it to human use, especially that of the worker. The economic order becomes completely independent of the ethical order. This could be carried very far. If profit is the only motive and there is no ethics involved, then the only problem with cheating in producing a product would not be the people it might harm but the fact that it might lead to less profit.

Solidarity in economics is the reaction against man who resists having the value of his work degraded to that of a machine. Work is ethically necessary for human perfection for three reasons: it makes family life and upkeep possible; it makes education possible, which realizes one of the main purposes of the family; and it aids the purpose of the state in preparing responsible citizens and ensuring domestic peace.

Papal Teaching on Morality in the Workplace

Many people find the teaching of the Catholic Church on the morality of economic order hard to understand, as it affirms neither strict liberal capitalism nor Marxism. An examination of the papal encyclicals is imperative to understand this. The principle that underlies papal teaching is that property and labor both have an individual and social dimension, both of which must be affirmed. As is the case with all rights, each includes corresponding duties.

When Leo XIII first sought to apply papal teaching to the problem of capital and labor in 1891, he was primarily motivated by the desire to give a moral direction to an economic climate that had become increasingly dominated by subjecting man to the machine. This situation had led to an adversarial relationship between capital and labor. The source of the conflict was the use entrepreneurs made of laborers in which they tried to make the maximum profit for the lowest possible wage. This did not recognize the subjective character of work. "In fact, in the final analysis it is always man who is the purpose of work, whatever work it is that is done by man — even if the common scale of values rates it as the merest 'service,' as the most monotonous, even the most alienating work."[187] This led to the Marxist reaction in which idealists tried to resolve this class conflict by eliminating property. The primary goal of this movement was to eliminate property as the source of the evil of exploitation.

Leo XIII gave the principles on which all future discussion of this matter has been based in *Rerum Novarum*. The Church's solution runs a middle course between liberal capitalism, with profit as the only motive and supply and demand as the only law, and Marxism, which seeks to resolve this materialist attitude by the equally materialistic attitude of class struggle, producing a freedom of the means of production unleashing matter. This latter idea was based on historical determinism and the total denial of human individuality.

Leo first upheld the right to private property as natural but then also pointed out that this right has the corresponding duty of social development. He then denied the *laissez-faire* capitalism of the nineteenth century, in which economics was based on the deterministic law of supply and demand. He also affirmed that, though the State could make laws about property and business, it could only play a supplementary role in these. For instance, the State could nationalize an industry like the railroads in a time of emergency, such as a war. However, when the emergency passed, ownership had to be returned to the private sector according to the principle of subsidiarity. Third, he recalled the duties of workers to employers for a just day's work. But he also demanded a salary for such work that recognized that a human being has done this work. The salary was thus declared to be a moral and human problem and not just a commodity to be bought and sold in the market. Finally, the pope condemned the class struggle as unnatural but also recognized

[187] Ibid.

the rights of workers to organize and form unions even if these excluded the employers. The strike is also implicitly recognized, although two principles must be affirmed for it to be morally good: it must be non-violent and it must not be an expression of class warfare. In other words, the final purpose of the strike must be to encourage the employers to act like employers and not simply to defeat them.

Later popes have developed these ideals further. At first, labor unions were only tolerated and Catholics were encouraged to only join Catholic unions. In *Quadragesimo Anno*, Pius XI approved non-confessional unions. He defended the guild system concept, which was protectionist and also was composed of both employers and workers, but he also affirmed the right of workers to defend their rights to guarantee a just wage. He said that a Christian could not accept the concept of class warfare and thus repudiated Marx. He also underlined the dangers of monopolies, which led to economic dictatorship. In response to Fascism, Nazism, and totalitarianism in general, the pope condemned State interference or ownership of the economic order. He further clarified that the just wage should be a family wage.

In *Mater et Magistra*, Pope St. John XXIII encouraged state intervention if it stimulates the economy, but not state substitution. Paul VI also taught in *Progressio Populorum* that the social question could no longer be localized in individual states but had taken on an international context. World peace demanded that all the nations embrace a kind of state cooperation and that individual societies recognize that what affects one has an influence on another.

In *Laborem Exercens*, this teaching is developed in a theoretical way and the pope specifically states that labor ("the broader multitude of people who lack these" [means of production])[188] is prior to capital ("the small but highly influential group of entrepreneurs, owners, and

---

[188] Ibid., no. 11.

holders of the means of production").[189] John Paul II points out that in the beginning of the Industrial Revolution, capital not only became separated from labor but was viewed in opposition to it. This led to a hardening of positions in which man was left out of the picture as the purpose for work. This in turn fostered the error of economism (human labor solely as an economic commodity), which is based on a materialistic philosophy that does not include the soul. Though the Marxist collective solution of denial of private property cannot be embraced, as it is anti-personal, neither can an exaggerated capitalism. The pope evokes Thomas Aquinas in two instances to correct these notions. The first is that capitalists should not be in opposition to labor but "should serve labor, and thus, by serving labor, they should make possible the achievement of the first principle of this order, namely, the universal destination of goods and the right of common use of them."[190] The second is that "the Church's teaching has always expressed the strong and deep conviction that man's work concerns not only the economy but also, and especially, personal values.... This is the principal reason in favor of the private ownership of the means of production."[191]

As for workers' rights, John Paul II invokes a distinction between direct employers, indirect employers, and workers. The direct employer "is the person or institution with whom the worker enters directly into a work contract."[192] The indirect employers are based on other factors that affect the employer-worker relationship. Though indirect employers are not specifically involved in the contracts and labor, they do bear a moral responsibility for the ethical nature of the business relationship. The State is an indirect employer. Given the complicated nature of modern economies in employer-state

[189] Ibid., no. 12.
[190] Ibid., no. 14.
[191] Ibid., no. 15.
[192] Ibid., no. 17.

relations, many may still see maximum profit as the goal. But since all property has a human dimension, "the objective rights of the worker ... must constitute the adequate and fundamental criterion for shaping the whole economy."[193] John Paul reaffirms former papal teaching in this regard that a just wage is the family wage, "a single salary given to the head of the family for his work, sufficient for the needs of the family without the other spouse having to take up gainful employment outside the home."[194]

The pope also recognizes that to safeguard the just wage and also to get employers to truly act as employers, workers have a right to organize in unions. But these unions cannot be an expression of class warfare motivated by "group or class 'egoism.' "[195] They cannot be based on class antagonism, let alone used as political weapons. The strike cannot descend to violence or the destruction of the political social order in such a way that it affects goods that are necessary for the pursuit of the common good of civil society.

Instead, morally, trade unionism and the strike must be an attempt by labor to get capital to act in the human interests of all concerned. In other words, it is an attempt to ensure that everyone participates in the common use of goods, which is a more primordial right than property. Pope Francis recognizes this point by maintaining that the union must appeal to the conscience of the business owner: "The conscience of the entrepreneur is the essential place in which that search happens. In particular, the Christian entrepreneur is asked to contrast the Gospel always with the reality in which he operates; and the Gospel asks him to put in the first place the human person and the common good, to do his part so that there are opportunities of

---

[193] Ibid.
[194] Ibid., no. 19.
[195] Ibid., no. 20.

work, of fitting work. Naturally, this enterprise cannot be carried out in isolation, but collaborating with others who share the ethical base and seek to widen the network as much as possible."[196]

This is the sense of the call of Pope Francis for redistribution of wealth. This is not to be understood in the sense of a government-mandated socialism that takes profits from companies and practices State ownership to simply provide welfare. It is a realistic attempt to introduce the fact that work is not an end nor is man simply a utilitarian means to profit. Instead, this forms perfect continuity with papal teaching, which has always sought to demonstrate that there is a social duty that goes along with wealth. This is the duty to provide a just product and pay a just wage. This is another affirmation of the emphasis the Church places on the spiritual character of human work and the denial of materialism.

Summary of Rights and Duties in the Economic Order

Church teaching on the economic order may be summarized using the encyclical of John Paul II, *Centesimus Annus*:

1. The dignity of work is a direct result of the spiritual nature of man. This involves not only the right to work but also the social character of work in relation to the family and the common good of State.

2. The right to private property is not an absolute right, as it entails the corresponding duty to develop property for the universal destination of human goods.

3. The right to establish professional associations of employers with workers or of workers alone is

[196] Pope Francis, Address to the *Centesimus Annus Pro Pontifice* Foundation (May 14, 2014), quoted in Zenit, Internet News Service.

affirmed. The State must not frustrate this right. The corresponding duty is always that this right is not based on class warfare but to encourage and ensure class cooperation.

4. There is a right to limitation of working hours, legitimate rest, and the right of women and children to just working conditions.

5. These are all founded on the right to a just wage, which "cannot be left to the free consent of the parties, so that the employer having paid what is agreed upon, has done his part and seemingly is not called upon to do anything beyond."[197] In this context, John Paul II also maintains that though these words were originally written in 1891, an era he describes as the time of "unbridled capitalism,"[198] they are just as current today. It is clear that Pope Francis was not the first to attack unrestrained profit as the only motive for economics. He is accused of having taught socialism by using the phrase "unbridled capitalism" in *Evangelii Gaudium*. Even though this phrase does not occur anywhere in this document, all the popes have warned about the economic and moral dangers of the unrestrained profit motive. Leo XIII and John Paul II could hardly be accused of being socialists.

---

[197] John Paul II, encyclical letter *Centesimus Annus* (May 1, 1991), no. 8, quoting Leo XIII, *Rerum Novarum*, no. 129.
[198] John Paul II, *Centesimus Annus*, no. 8.

Epilogue

Three Basic Human Societies

There are thus three basic societies necessary for the perfection of man in Christian social order. They may be summarized as follows:

First is the family, the most basic community. Its final purpose is the procreation and education of children and the mutual perfection of the spouses. In the family that results from the sacrament of the New Testament, it is also the principle means of holiness for the spouses. The order needed to attain this end is openness to life, freedom of choice regarding education, and mutual relationship of the spouses. This relationship involves the necessity of indissolubility because the spouse becomes a second self in the full meaning of that term. The economic order is necessary for providing for the physical and spiritual needs of all family members. Authority in the family is exercised by the parents according to their natural relationship to the procreation and education of children.

One purpose in writing this book was to demonstrate that the family is the most basic cell of society. It is also the one most under attack today, especially from the State. This occurs through the economic order, where exaggerated socialism leads to the reduction of the freedom and identity of parents. The State seeks to become the parent community. Incorrect applications of ideas like "it takes a village to raise a child" shift the whole emphasis from the family as a community, which has certain specified rights and duties, in the direction of common ownership of children and state education, completely disregarding school choice or curriculum. Though the State does have a concern for marriage and family, following the principles invoked in this book, especially organic growth and subsidiarity, this concern is supplemental, not primary. To the extent that the State tries to force solutions on the family (though perhaps well-meaning about education and number of children and the like) without any due regard for the freedom and rights of the parents, both communities suffer.

In Europe, one problematic social area of the relation of the family and State is that of euthanasia. The Church is clear that this is always gravely evil and an assault on the right to life, the most basic human right. Regardless of the consequences for medical ethics, the impact on the family is problematic. Care for the elderly is becoming more difficult as people live longer. The modern nuclear family is being forced back into the extended family because of economic concerns. Care of the elderly and unemployment for the young place great social burdens on the household. In some cases, parents complain that they are forced to care for their grown children who have substance abuse issues but will not contribute to or obey the rule of the home. Social agencies are often overwhelmed by the sheer number of psychologically and physically impaired individuals.

Again, prudence and justice must govern this situation. The State cannot interfere by using "death panels" or, in the extreme, even child euthanasia, which is murder. On the other hand, realistic palliative care should be clearly defined. Instead of living wills, which often leave medical decisions to professionals with no real interest in what the patient wants and place economic considerations over moral principles, durable powers of attorney should be encouraged. In these, the patient chooses someone who knows and approves his values to make decisions about his health.

Principles should also guide parents for adult children. They should not just be allowed to pursue a course of perpetual adolescence or indolence. Nor should their every behavior be tolerated. If they can contribute to the family in any way, it is a recognition of their freedom as persons and an encouragement of their responsibility as adults to require them to do so. If the adult child persists in flaunting the rules, then he must be forced to leave the home and do his best to earn what living he can. This is not a lack of love or justice but an implementation of it. Unless prompted by pressing family needs, living at home for those who are intelligent and able-bodied adults should be a temporary measure and not prolonged unduly. Otherwise, parents run the risk of never allowing their sons or daughters to properly develop as responsible adults.

The State, the second society in traditional teaching, has peace and justice in the temporal order as its final purpose. The order necessary to attain such an end is a constitution, whether written or unwritten, in which human laws are made that apply the natural law. The authority structure that makes and executes such laws is any form that is just. This could be a monarchy, aristocracy, democracy, or a combination of the three. The criterion for determining if this authority structure is effective is based on how much this authority pursues the common good rather than its private good or sacrifices the common good for the private good of authority. The former is a just government; the latter, a tyranny.

As the State becomes larger and technology shrinks the world more and more, social problems become very complex. The large bureaucracies and media development demanded by the modern State open immense possibilities for social interaction and understanding, but they are also the occasion of great injustice. Perhaps there have never been simple solutions to complex political and moral issues, but today the very magnitude of the people involved makes this fact even more complicated. Justice must be based on objective human nature and on the agreed constitution of the State for there to be true social peace and progress.

One example of the moral and social complexity facing the modern State is immigration. This, coupled with the multiculturalism it brings, is a great moral problem in both Europe and North America. The Church has been at pains to emphasize that justice demands welcoming the stranger. Practically, however, a State also has a right and duty to preserve its sovereignty and freedom as a given nation, which includes the right to protect its borders from incursion, be it military or individual. This would include the duty to acknowledge the just treatment of offenders and not use undue force to do so.

This duty of the State would include a realistic assessment of the multicultural threat that one culture could make on another — for instance, the sheer difficulty of integrating sharia law into the traditional understanding of Western democracy. If the principles of one culture, even a religious one, essentially involve the overthrow of the State, the constitution, and the way of life practiced by the citizens, then whether war is declared or not, this is an unjust incursion into the State and must be resisted. If the concern is economic, then steps should be taken to integrate the new population into the economy, always preserving the indigenous workforce. With some mass migrations, solutions are very muddy. Still, the rights and duties of everyone, as well as the established law, must be either respected or modified to meet new situations.

The Church, the third society, is also necessary for the pursuit of the good. The final goal of the Church is the Beatific Vision of Heaven.

The Church is only perfected in the communion of saints in Heaven. The order necessary to attain this end is a sacramental one because it is an extension of the human nature of Christ throughout time and space. The authority structure that preserves this order is not the same as the State because the end and sanction behind this order is supernatural. The proper authority structure to attain this order is thus a hierarchy founded by Christ that acts in His name to serve the members of the Church here on earth by teaching the truth and promoting grace and morals through the sacraments.

The incursion of the State on the rights of the Church must be resisted. This does not always involve active dissent, but it sometimes demands recognition of an impasse between the two and the toleration of an imperfect situation. The principles invoked in this book even allow for two different levels of the same social relationship.

One example is gay marriage. Obviously, the Church can never approve this in any way. It is contrary to both the natural law and revealed law. However, given that the modern nanny state looks on itself increasingly as the origin of all values based on whatever is the politically correct philosophy of the moment, an almost unavoidable political collision seems to be coming on this issue.

A good example would be an "established" church in Europe forced by the State to perform gay weddings in church by order of parliament. The minster may refuse to do this because he has qualms of conscience. However, if he does so, the bishop must provide another minister to perform the "wedding." Many people think that this may eventually be the case in other countries because performing weddings is often viewed as a "business." Those putting on weddings are, therefore, required to observe the anti-discrimination laws of every business. Religious institutions that adhere to traditional Judeo-Christian moral principles must either comply or no longer be about the business of performing weddings regarded as legal by the civil law. "Equality" is being reinterpreted (as C. S. Lewis described it in his assessment of democracy quoted in the introduction of this book) as the fact that all lifestyles are equal and so must be legally recognized. A moral solution to this problem would be that the Church simply gets out of the civil marriage "business" and there would be two weddings, one legal and one religious. There are many countries in which this is the case.

Only a few of the modern problems facing the family, the State, and the Church are briefly outlined above. What should be evident from the principles and applications treated in this book, however, is that if social peace is to ever be attained in this world, this can only be based on a social order that recognizes all the levels on which a human being can be happy and fulfilled. Catholic social teaching has always taken pains to do justice to all forms of human fulfillment. This has led to affirmation that both the order and the end on which each society is formed must conform to human nature. This also entails a respect, recognition, and promotion of each of these three societies in their distinction and, at the same time, their mutual relationship.